KU-714-405

The Making of the 20th Century

This series of specially commissioned titles focuses attention on significant and often controversial events and themes of world history in the present century. The authors, many of them already outstanding in their field, have tried to close the gap between the intelligent layman, whose interest is aroused by recent history, and the specialist student at university. Each book will therefore provide sufficient narrative and explanation for the newcomer while offering the specialist student detailed source-references and bibliographies, together with interpretation and reassessment in the light of recent scholarship.

In the choice of subjects there will be a balance between breadth in some spheres and detail in others; between the essentially political and matters scientific, economic or social. The series cannot be a comprehensive account of everything that has happened in the twentieth century, but it will provide a guide to recent research and explain something of the times of extraordinary change and complexity in which we live.

The Making of the 20th Century

Series Editor: CHRISTOPHER THORNE

Titles in the Series include

Already published

Titles in preparation include

The Ottoman Empire and its Successors

Peter Mansfield

Macmillan

First published 1973 by
THE MACMILLAN PRESS LTD
London and Basingstoke
Associated companies in New York Dublin
Melbourne Johannesburg and Madras

SBN 333 03663 8 (hard cover)
333 07382 7 (paper cover)

Printed in Great Britain by
HAZELL WATSON AND VINEY LTD
Aylesbury, Bucks

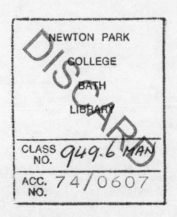

Contents

Abbreviations

I.B.R.D.	International Bank for Reconstruction and Development
Antonius	George Antonius, *The Arab Awakening: the Story of the Arab National Movement* (Beirut, 1962)
Lewis	Bernard Lewis, *The Emergence of Modern Turkey* (2nd edition, London, 1968)
Hurewitz i and ii	J. C. Hurewitz, *Diplomacy in the Near and Middle East.* Vol. i 1535–1914 and vol. ii 1914–1956 (Princeton, 1956)

Preface

THIS book attempts to outline the social, political and economic development of the western half of the Islamic world during this century. Apart from the Turkish Republic, which rose from the ashes of the Ottoman Empire, the story mainly concerns the fate of the former Arab provinces of the Empire, although it also refers to Iran, with its close affinities of religion, culture and historical experience to both Turks and Arabs.

For the transliteration of Arab, Turkish and Persian names I have generally made use of all the forms familiar to the non-specialist where possible.

I am much indebted to Derek Hopwood, Librarian of St Antony's College Middle East Centre, for help in preparing the Bibliography.

P. M.

Acknowledgements

THE author and publisher thank the following for permission to reproduce the photographs which appear on the jacket and cover : President Kemal Atatürk (by courtesy of the Turkish Embassy, London), President Bourguiba (by courtesy of the Tunisian Embassy, London), King Feisal I (Radio Times–Hulton Picture Library), President Nasser (Radio Times–Hulton Picture Library).

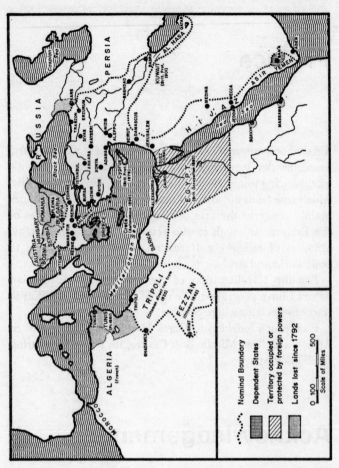

I   The Ottoman Empire in 1908

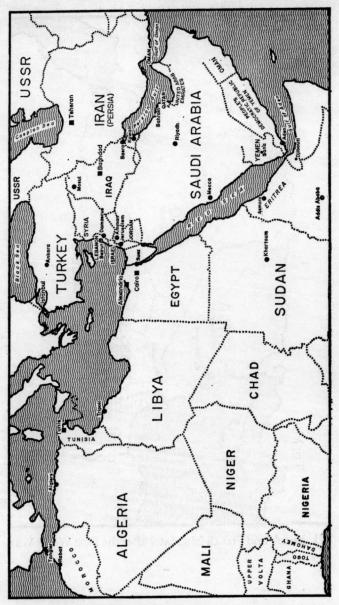

II The Middle East and North Africa at the Present Day

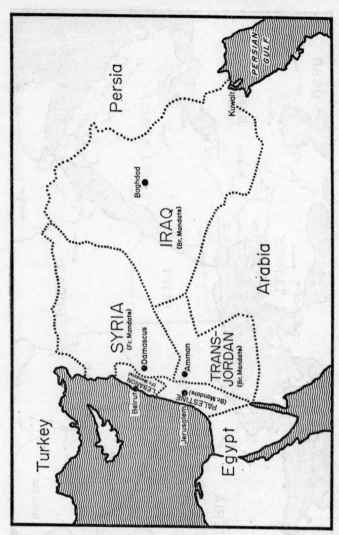

III British and French Mandates after the First World War

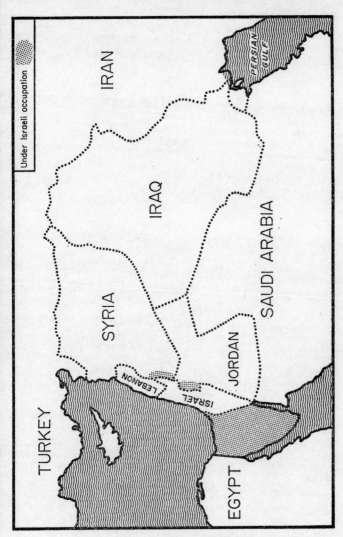

IV   Arab States and Israel 1973

1 The Background

THE Islamic religion was founded by Muhammad (died
A.D. 632), who was an Arab of the Hashim family of the
Quraish tribe, which occupied the flourishing commercial
town of Mecca near the west central coast of present-day
Saudi Arabia. Muhammad was a political genius who united
western Arabia, the Hejaz; by the time he died he had laid
the foundation for the unification of the whole peninsula.

Islam is an Arabic word meaning 'submission' to the will
of God, and it is used in two senses; first, as the religion of
those who believe in the mission of the Prophet Muhammad
as the final revelation of God's will to humanity, and in the
Koran as God's word transmitted to mankind through his
Prophet; and second, the social, cultural, legal and political
system that has grown up around the Islamic religion.

The early history of Islam is that of the Arab conquests
shortly after the death of Muhammad; his Muslim Arab
followers burst out of Arabia to overrun the great but
decadent empires of Persia and Byzantium. To the north
they swept through Syria into Turkey to threaten Constantinople. To the east they conquered Iraq, Persia, Afghanistan
and crossed the River Oxus into Turkestan. To the west
they took Egypt and the whole of North Africa and, having
reached the Atlantic, turned north through Spain into
southern and central France. Within a century of the
Prophet's death an Arab empire had been established, which
stretched from present-day Portugal in the west to the River
Indus in the east.

These military conquests had been swift and spectacular,

and it was not surprising that the unity of such an extended empire did not survive for long. By A.D. 850 the central power had largely been usurped by provincial governors. But what was of lasting historical importance was the new civilisation imparted by the conquerors. Two processes, which were linked but not identical, were at work : Islamisation and Arabisation.

In every country that the Arabs conquered the great majority of the population—Christian, Jewish, Zoroastrian or pagan—embraced Islam. The Islamic faith is a strict monotheism. Muslims recognise the divine origin of the Old and New Testaments and are enjoined to tolerate Jews and Christians as possessors of a divine revelation, although an incomplete one. Christians and Jews held positions of considerable power and influence within the Islamic Empire but they could not achieve full equality of status. They had to pay special taxes and were not allowed to serve in the army. Pagans and polytheists, on the other hand, were given the choice of conversion to Islam, slavery or death.

Schisms appeared in Islam shortly after Muhammad's death. His followers elected a successor (Arabic *Khalifa* or Caliph), but violent factional disputes soon arose between them. The fourth Caliph, the Prophet's son-in-law Ali, was forced to abdicate and later murdered. This gave rise to the principal division within Islam—the majority of Sunnis, who accept the orthodox Caliphs, and the minority of Shias, who believe that Ali was the true successor to Muhammad. Iran today is the principal Muslim country in which Shia Islam is the religion of the state.

The process of Arabisation had preceded Islam. From the second century B.C. Arab tribes had moved out of Arabia into Syria and Iraq where they settled and became absorbed. The influence of their culture and language was limited until it was allied to the great force of Islam in the seventh century A.D. The decadent Hellenistic and Persian cultures of Syria, Egypt and Mesopotamia gave way to the new dynamic faith. Arabisation had two elements : linguistic as the conquered peoples acquired the Arabic language, and racial whereby the Arab invaders mixed their blood with the indigenous population. As a consequence the very term 'Arab' came to change its meaning.[1] Originally it had referred only to the nomadic tribesmen (bedouin) of Arabia, but over the centuries it came to refer to all the Arabised people who made up the Arab world in its modern sense. The older meaning lingered on and until recent times the term 'Arab' was used in settled communities to refer to the desert nomads. But gradually the wider meaning of Arab predominated until today it generally refers to anyone who speaks Arabic.

The degree of racial Arabisation was stronger in some parts of the modern Arab world than others. It was more intense in Syria where it preceded Islam than in Egypt where it did not, and a substantial Christian majority—the Copts—adopted the Arabic language while remaining racially separate. There were also large minority communities in the Arab world—such as the Berbers in North Africa and the Kurds of northern Iraq—who resisted both the linguistic and, to a large extent, the racial elements of Arabisation.

Islamisation and Arabisation, as we have seen, were closely linked but the former was ultimately much the more extensive. The Muslim faith spread far beyond the Arab world into Persia, Turkey, East, Central and West Africa, China, India and South-East Asia. Yet the link between Islam and Arabism remained. Because of the lack of racial barriers in Islam there was considerable racial intermingling —especially in Persia, Turkey and parts of black Africa. The Turkish and Persian languages (especially Persian) contain many Arabic loan-words, and Persian is still written in the Arabic script. Moreover the Koran is written in Arabic, and the twin holy cities of Islam—Mecca and Medina—are in Arabia. It is one of the duties of a Muslim believer to

make the pilgrimage (*hajj*) to them at least once in his life-
time.

Some thirty years after the Prophet's death a member of
the Umayya family of Mecca secured the Caliphate and
founded the Umayyad dynasty which ruled from Damascus
(661–750). The Umayyads were overthrown by a new
dynasty, the Abbasids (750–1258), who established themselves in Iraq and founded Baghdad as their capital. Persians
played a predominant role in their empire, which reached
a high peak of civilisation but soon began to break up
administratively. In the tenth century rival caliphates were
established by the Fatimid dynasty in Egypt and North
Africa and by the survivors of the Umayyads ruling in
Spain. In the middle of the eleventh century Persia was
overrun by Seljuq Turks, Muslims from Central Asia, who
entered Baghdad in 1055 and eventually established an
empire from India to the Aegean.

The Abbasid Caliphs retained their title as overlords, but
by the middle of the ninth century they had already lost
most of their power to provincial governors who were frequently Turkish mercenaries. It was the Turks, as central
Asian converts to Islam, who ultimately provided the strong
political framework which the Islamic Empire established
by the Arabs had previously lacked. They entered the Islamic
world first as slaves and then as mercenary adventurers. In
1258 the Mongol invasion which brought the Abbasid Caliphate to an end also destroyed the Seljuq Sultanate in Asia
Minor, but before the end of the century the foundations of
the Ottoman Empire had been laid on its ruins by Othman,
a Turkish mercenary recently converted to Islam. He and
his successors gradually extended their rule throughout
Asia Minor and their influence into the Balkans, until in
1453 Mohammed II, 'the Conqueror', took Constantinople
and overthrew the Byzantine Empire.

It was Mohammed II's grandson, Selim I, who carried
on the process of empire-building. After a crushing victory

over the Shah of Persia in 1515 he turned south to overthrow the Mameluke Sultanate of Egypt which included
Syria and Palestine. While he was in Cairo a deputation
from the Sharif of Mecca came to offer him the Keys of the
Holy City and the title of Protector of the Holy Places. He
also assumed the title of Caliph of Islam, although this was
of lesser importance at the time, and it was not until the
eighteenth century that his successors made use of the claim
to universal leadership of the Muslim world.[2]

Selim I's successor, Soliman the Magnificent (1520–66),
developed the best fleet in the Mediterranean and extended
his rule along North Africa to include Algiers, Tunis, Tripoli
and Oran. By Soliman's death the Ottoman Empire included nearly all the Arab world except Morocco in the far
west. Virtually all of Sunni Islam of that period (excluding
India) was united under Turkish rule against Persia, where
a Shia dynasty, the Safavids, had established itself at the
beginning of the sixteenth century. For the next two centuries the Turkish and Persian Empires continued to dispute
for control of Mesopotamia (Iraq) until finally it came
under Ottoman rule.

The European dominions of Turkey reached their greatest
extent in the second half of the sixteenth century when the
island of Crete at last surrendered to the Turkish forces.
These dominions then included all of present-day Romania,
Yugoslavia, Greece, Bulgaria, Albania and Cyprus as well as
part of Hungary, Poland and Russia's Crimean coast. But
although the frontiers of the Empire remained almost unchanged until the end of the eighteenth century its decline
from the peak of its inner strength had already begun much
earlier, before the end of the sixteenth century. 'If the first
ten sultans of the house of Osman astonish us with the
spectacle of a series of able and intelligent men rare if not
unique in the annals of dynastic succession, the remainder
of the rulers of that line provides an even more astonishing
series of incompetents, degenerates and misfits.'[3] The de-

cline in the quality of the Empire's rulers was largely due to
the practice initiated by Soliman the Magnificent of eliminating all political rivals in the sultan's family. After
Mohammed III had inaugurated his reign in 1595 by the
murder of nineteen brothers the heirs to the throne were
kept in protective isolation in the Palace, with the result
that they lacked the administrative experience as provincial
governors that had been earned by earlier sultans. There
was a fatal deterioration in the quality of the Empire's administration, which became increasingly corrupt and inefficient. There was an even more disastrous decline in the
quality of the Turkish armed forces, which had once been
the terror of Europe.

While the Ottoman Empire decayed from within the
pressures upon it from outside were becoming more powerful and insistent. A new phase in the long struggle between
Islam and western Christendom was beginning. The first,
which had started with the Arab conquests, had lasted for
about one thousand years and had generally been to Islam's
advantage. Although the tide began to turn in Spain and
Sicily in the eleventh century Islam was the more powerful
around the southern and eastern shores of the Mediterranean. The medieval Christian crusades for the recovery of
the Holy Land ended in failure, and for at least the first
half of the thousand-year period Islam was the superior
civilisation. Abbasid Baghdad was a great centre of civilisation at a time when western Europe was in the Dark Ages.
The final loss of Spain to the Catholic kings at the end of the
fifteenth century was offset by the Turkish conquest of Constantinople in 1453 and the Ottoman expansion into
Christian south-eastern Europe. Although twice reaching
the gates of Vienna the Ottomans never succeeded in taking
it, and in 1683 the tide was clearly seen to have turned with
a major defeat of the Turkish forces by King John Sobieski
of Poland.

Of equal importance to western and central Europe's

gradual winning of military supremacy over the Turks was
its rise in commercial power. The opening of a new trade
route to Asia via the Cape by the Portuguese in the sixteenth
century and the establishment of Dutch and British power in
Asia in the seventeenth century 'deprived Turkey of the
greater part of her foreign commerce and left her, together
with the countries over which she ruled, in a stagnant back-
water through which the life-giving stream of world trade no
longer flowed'.[4] At the same time the flood of cheap silver
from the Spanish colonies in the New World caused a violent
inflation, and disastrous devaluation of the currency of the
Ottoman Empire. The consequent economic distress was
compounded by the government's increasing demands for
revenues from the already overtaxed peasantry for the
swelling bureaucracy and armed forces. While the economies
of the European powers made rapid progress in the seventeenth and eighteenth centuries, that of the Ottoman Empire
actually declined. Agriculture deteriorated as the peasantry
abandoned the countryside for the towns, but there was no
compensating development of industry. Turkey's stagnant
science and technology lagged increasingly behind the west,
and it lacked any independent entrepreneurial class which
might have led an industrial revolution. Western economic
superiority was also manifested within the Ottoman Empire.
In the sixteenth century, when the Empire was at the height
of its powers, the Ottoman sultan granted special privileges
to the French, English, Venetians and other non-Muslims,
who had established themselves within the Empire to trade.
These privileges—known as the Capitulations—exempted
them from taxes imposed on Muslim Ottoman subjects and
gave them the right to be tried in their own consular courts.
As Ottoman power declined the privileges were reinforced.
By the nineteenth century there were flourishing European
business communities in many parts of the Empire which
were virtually above the law. There were similar Capitulations in Persia, China, Japan and many parts of Asia.

In the eighteenth century the sultans began to place increasing emphasis on their claim to the caliphate. The Empire was run as an Islamic military autocracy with the Sultan–Caliph at its head. The non-Muslim subjects of the Empire, who were mostly Christians, were organised in *millets* or religious minority communities with internal autonomy and considerable individual and communal freedom. In contrast to the early centuries of Islam, however, Christians were not always exempt from military service. Periodically they were conscripted to the Janissaries, who formed the shock troops of the Ottoman armies. Some of them were appointed as court officials and the most promising were trained to run the administration. Non-Muslims achieved positions of considerable power and influence, but supreme authority always remained in the hands of the Sultan.

The Turks were not totally unaware of the dangers of falling behind the West. Since the Empire was based on military power they were most ready to borrow or imitate western military techniques. But other manifestations of western technology, such as printing, were originally proscribed by the 'ulema' (the Muslim scholars and legal experts) as contrary to Islam. The sultans and the religious authorities were understandably appalled by the egalitarian ideas of the French Revolution with their overtones of atheism, but they were unable to immunise the Empire from their influence. Bonaparte's invasion of Egypt in 1798, although it may be counted a military failure, not only marked the first step in the process of Europe's dismemberment of the Ottoman Empire, but planted the seeds of revolutionary ideas within the body of Islam.

The first conscious attempts to catch up with the West had been taken in the early eighteenth century when printing was introduced despite the doubts of the *ulema*, and reforms in the military and naval training introduced. These were pursued by Sultan Selim III (1789–1807) and his

successor Mahmud III (1808–39), who freed his hands by
massacring the increasingly rebellious Janissaries in 1826.
Early and mid-nineteenth century reforms covered education, the legal system, and the government bureaucracy, as
well as the armed forces. Some of these reforms were im-
aginative and far-sighted, but the sultans and their ministers
were restricted at every turn by the need to adapt them to
the tenets of Islam. Their great failure was in finance and
economics; none of them succeeded in balancing the budget
or restoring Turkey's financial credit abroad.

The nineteenth-century Ottoman reforms did not succeed
in arresting the decline of the Empire. A turning-point had
been reached in 1774 when, following a defeat at the hands
of the Russians, the Sultan had to concede to Catherine the
Great the right of protector of all his Orthodox Christian
subjects. In 1775 Bukovina was lost to Austria, and Bess-
arabia to Russia in 1812. In 1799 the Sultan had sent an
Albanian force to Egypt to help expel the French invaders.
Muhammad Ali, an officer in this force, had subsequently
made himself master of Egypt and was recognised as Viceroy by the Sultan in 1805. Muhammad Ali and his son,
Ibrahim Pasha, were political and military leaders of high
calibre. With Turkish officers and Egyptian peasants
(fellahin) as soldiers they fashioned a powerful army, which
eventually shook the Ottoman Empire to its foundations. In
answer to the Sultan's entreaties, Muhammad Ali sent troops
to Arabia to quell the fanatically puritanical Islamic revival
movement of the Wahhabis, who were contesting the Sultan–
Caliph's authority over the Holy Places. Having placed the
Sultan in his debt, Muhammad Ali turned south to colonise
the Sudan and, after securing control of both shores of the
Red Sea, returned to the Sultan's assistance. This time
Ibrahim Pasha came to suppress an insurrection in Greece.
He was initially successful, but the British and Russian fleets
intervened to defeat the combined Egyptian and Turkish
navies at Navarino in 1827, and the Greeks secured their

independence five years later. This did nothing to restrain the ambitions of Muhammad Ali and Ibrahim Pasha. When the Sultan refused Ibrahim Pasha the governorship of Syria as a reward for his assistance, he proceeded to seize it and was formally recognised by the Sultan in 1833. When his armies went further to threaten Constantinople, the Powers of Europe again intervened to save the Sultan who was obliged in return to sign the humiliating treaty of Hunkiar Iskelessi (1833),[5] which not only gave Russia the right to intervene in Turkish affairs, but included a secret clause permitting Russia to insist on the closing of the Dardanelles in the event of war. The London Conference of Austria, France, Britain, Prussia and Russia, held in 1839 on Britain's initiative, put a final curb on Muhammad Ali's ambitions and forced him to abandon Syria, although retaining the hereditary viceroyalty of Egypt.[6]

Britain's action in coming to the Sultan's assistance against Muhammad Ali was consistent with its Near Eastern policy first established by William Pitt in 1791 : to prevent the disintegration of the Ottoman Empire in case its ports should fall into more dangerous, especially Russian, hands. British statesmen were primarily concerned with any threat to their Indian possessions, and would have regarded Russian expansion into the eastern Mediterranean with the greatest alarm. This was the motive behind the alliance of the British (and French) with Turkey against Russia in the Crimean War (1853–4). For similar reasons Lord Palmerston, who presided over British foreign policy in the mid-nineteenth century, strongly opposed the building of a Suez Canal. Control of the Canal by a foreign power would be a deadly danger and he correctly foresaw that Britain might have to occupy Egypt to prevent it.

The fact that the Powers of Europe were needed to preserve the Sick Man of Europe from destruction merely increased their influence and dominance in Constantinople. The sultans were reduced to the strategy of playing one rival power against the other as best they could. In 1861, following a brief but savage civil war between Christians, Muslims and Druzes in Syria, the French had landed troops in Beirut and the Powers imposed a settlement providing for autonomy within the Empire for the predominantly Christian inhabitants of Mount Lebanon.[7]

Following the Russo-Turkish war of 1877, in which the Russians attacked with the avowed purpose of winning freedom for the Slav people of the Ottoman Empire,* Turkey had to sign the humiliating Treaty of San Stefano. This was set aside by the Cyprus Convention of 1878[8] which stripped Turkey of much of her territory in Europe. In return for British protection against further Russian encroachments the Sultan had to promise to England 'to introduce necessary reforms, to be agreed upon later between the two powers, into the government, and for the protection of the Christian and other subjects of the Porte † in these territories'. Also, although the Powers may have wanted the head of the Empire to survive, they had little compunction about detaching some of its outer members when it served their interests.

France took Algiers in 1830 and went on to conquer the interior. In 1881 French rule spread to Tunisia and in the following year Britain occupied Egypt. Although the Sultan's suzerainty was still acknowledged, Britain effectively ruled Egypt for the next fifty years. During the nineteenth century Britain also established herself on the southern and eastern shores of the Arabian peninsula where Ottoman authority had never fully extended. The Persian Gulf (like the Suez Canal when it was opened in 1869) was

* It was the savage Ottoman suppression of the Bulgars which aroused the indignation of William Gladstone and reduced the Liberal Party's enthusiasm for the traditional British policy of maintaining Muslim Turkey as a bulwark against Christian Russia.

† The Ottoman government was usually referred to as the Sublime Porte – a reference to the gate at the entrance of the government buildings in Istanbul.

prized as a trade route and as a line of defence for India and British communications with the East. To forestall any attempt by Bonaparte to establish himself in the Gulf at the time when he was in occupation of Egypt, Britain concluded a treaty with the Ruler of Muscat in 1798.[9] From 1820 Britain concluded a series of treaties with other Arab rulers in the Gulf which placed them under British protection and provided for the exclusion of other Powers. Most of these treaties survived up to the 1970s.

By 1900 the Christian countries of the West had decisively gained the upper hand in their prolonged political and military struggle with the Islamic world. But the contest did not end there, for the Christian Powers—led by Britain and France—pressed home their victory. For all its weakness and decay, the Ottoman Empire was still a major power in nineteenth-century terms, even if the primary reason for its survival was that each of the western Powers wanted it to retain enough substance to act as a barrier to the ambitions of the rest. The peoples of the western half of the Islamic world—and even to some extent the Muslims of the Indian sub-continent after the decline of the Mogul Emperors—could look upon the Sultan–Caliph in Constantinople as the protector and preserver of the interests of the Muslim *umma* or nation. Ethnic divisions were not recognised by the Ottoman government. The Turks were politically dominant and Turkish was the language of government, but Arabic was the language of learning and law. No one could deny that the Prophet Muhammad was an Arab, the Holy Koran was written in Arabic and the Arabs had been the instrument through which Islam had conquered the world.[10] The first signs of change had come in the second half of the nineteenth century with the beginnings of the rise of the secular movement of Arab nationalism. Because the people of the Arab heartland—Arabia, Syria and Iraq—were under Turkish, and not western Christian, rule it was against the

Turks that the Arab national rebellion was ultimately directed.

The revolt succeeded in that Turkish domination of these Arab heartlands was ended, but it also failed because it did not give the Arabs the freedom and independence they sought. On the contrary, it enabled the western Powers to consolidate their hegemony over most of the rest of the Islamic lands which had so far escaped their control. Ironically, it was the core of the Ottoman Empire—Turkey, which had been rejected by the majority of its imperial subjects—that succeeded in preserving and consolidating its independence after its total defeat by the western Powers.

The central theme of this essay is the vast disappointment of the Arab peoples in the fruits of victory, their bitter sense of humiliation and their struggle to recover their dignity. It suggests why so much of their emotional, intellectual and physical energies have been devoted to this purpose and why in consequence the political and socio-economic reforms, which would have enabled them more easily to match the overbearing power of the West, have often been neglected. The aim is to propose reasons for the impression that has been gained in the West that the Arabs have failed to come to terms with the twentieth century and to assess how far this view is correct. At the same time an attempt will be made to compare the Arabs' experience with that of the other two peoples of the western Islamic world—the Turks and the Persians.

2 The Ottoman Empire 1900–1914

WHEN the twentieth century opened the Ottoman Empire was a reduced and ragged shadow of its former greatness. Most of the Muslim possessions in Africa and the Christian provinces in Europe had been lost. The Sublime Porte, with its empty treasury and corrupt and inefficient bureaucracy, confronted the overbearing power of the principal states of Europe and their ever-increasing imperial ambitions.

The man at the centre of the Empire, who in 1900 had already been Sultan for twenty-four years, was not without ability. Ultimately his policies could not have saved the Empire, but his cunning and shrewdness served to shore up the ramshackle structure for a time. When Abdul Hamid II came to the throne in 1876 he raised high hopes among his subjects as a devout but enlightened and liberal monarch. He appointed as Grand Vezir the prominent reforming statesman Midhat Pasha, who at once introduced a new constitution for the Empire, which reduced the autocratic powers of the Sultan and established the principle of demo-cratic equality for all his subjects. But it was not long before Abdul Hamid showed his true opinion of liberalism and democracy. He soon dismissed Midhat, but for the sake of appearances allowed the elections under the new constitu-tion to proceed, and the first Ottoman parliament actually met in March 1877 with deputies from all parts of the Empire. Instant democracy is a fiction, and the deputies, who were without parliamentary experience, had been elected under strong official pressure. Nevertheless they began to expose the widespread corruption and abuses of government officials. This was not Abdul Hamid's intention and within less than a year he had dissolved the chamber and suspended the constitution. It remained suspended for thirty years.

Although profoundly reactionary in his political views, Abdul Hamid, like his predecessors in the early nineteenth century, was not opposed to selected westernising reforms to strengthen what was left of his Empire. His primary aim was to reinforce its cohesion and unity, by diplomacy if possible and by repression if this failed.

The new administrative system aimed at uniformity and stronger centralised control in the hands of the Sultan's ministers in Istanbul.

The Empire was divided into provinces (*vilayet*) each of which was administered by a governor-general (*vali*) directly responsible to the central government in Constantinople. The vilayet was sub-divided into a number of counties (*sanjak*), each of which had at its head a lieutenant-governor (*mutasarref*) who was a subordinate of the vali's; while the sanjak was itself made up of numerous smaller units each of which was administered by an official (*qaimmaqam*) whose immediate chief was the mutasarref. In a few exceptional cases, a county which for some reason did not fit into the normal provincial scheme was created into a separate administrative entity known as an independent sanjak, which meant that its mutasarref enjoyed the prerogative of a vali so far as executive powers and direct reference to Constantinople went.[1]

Since 1861 the Sanjak of Lebanon had been autonomous in this manner.

In 1887 an administrative reorganisation of the Fertile Crescent had created the Vilayet of Aleppo in the north, the Vilayet of Beirut in the west, the Vilayet of Syria in the east, the autonomous Sanjak of the Lebanon detached from the centre of the Vilayet of Beirut and the autonomous Sanjak of Jerusalem to the south. Iraq was divided into the three Vilayets of Mosul, Baghdad and Basra. The Arabian peninsula, largely desert and inhabited by nomads, was only very loosely under Ottoman rule. In 1841 an attempt had been made to bring western Arabia (the Hejaz) into the centralised bureaucratic system by the appointment of a vali who shared his powers with the Arab Grand Sharifs, the traditional rulers of Mecca and Medina. In 1871 Turkish rule was extended by the occupation of al-Hasa in eastern Arabia and in 1872 a Turkish expedition had occupied Sanaa, the capital of mountainous Yemen. But large areas of the interior of the peninsula—notably the principalities of Nejd and Shammar ruled by the families of Ibn Saud and Ibn Rashid—were virtually independent, while Britain was the paramount power on the southern and eastern coasts of Arabia through its occupation of Aden and its treaty relationships with the Arab rulers of the small Persian Gulf Sheikhdoms. The once great Persian Empire, on the other hand, no longer presented any kind of threat to the Ottoman Sultan. It was militarily feeble and the corruption and inefficiency of its administration easily exceeded that of the Ottoman Empire. To raise revenues the Qajar shahs had mortgaged most of the country's natural resources to foreign powers, especially Britain and Russia. The partition of Persia into a British sphere of influence in the south and a Russian sphere in the north was to be formalized by the Anglo-Russian agreement of 1907.[2]

In North Africa Abdul Hamid's only remaining possession was Libya, divided into the Vilayets of Tripoli and Benghazi, and much of this was to be taken by Italy in 1912. France had consolidated its rule in Algeria (after forty years of relentless pacification) and in Tunisia. In both countries she was actively encouraging French settlement. Ultimately the 'assimilation' of these two predominantly Muslim territories to France was to prove an impossible ideal, but French rule was to give them an indelible French stamp. Morocco, which was never part of the Ottoman Empire and had survived the nineteenth century as a medieval Islamic fossil despite the

attempts at modernisation of its last great sultan, Moulay
Hassan (1873–94), was also occupied by France and declared
a French Protectorate in 1912 (except for a small area in
the north which was a Spanish Protectorate). Morocco,
therefore, joined Algeria and Tunisia to form what was
known as French North Africa throughout the first half of
the twentieth century.

British rule in Egypt was lighter in the sense that there
was no concerted attempt to Anglicise the country as France
was Gallicising North Africa. Consequently there was no
necessity for the nation's personality to reassert itself in its
subsequent bid for independence. But in practice British
authority was almost unqualified—especially when the com-
manding presence of Sir Evelyn Baring—later Lord Cromer
—(British Consul-General in Egypt 1883–1907), was there
to enforce it. Ottoman suzerainty over Egypt was nominally
recognised until 1914 when a British Protectorate was declared, but the Sultan had no practical influence in Egypt's
administration. The rights of other powers under the terms
of the Capitulations were a much more important limitation
to British rule in Egypt. In 1898, when the Sudan was re-
conquered from the followers of the Mahdi by an Anglo-
Egyptian force under Lord Kitchener, an Anglo-Egyptian
Condominium (devised by Cromer) was set up without
reference to the Porte.

In 1900 there had been none of the concerted uprisings of
the Arab provinces of the Ottoman Empire of the kind that
had occurred among its Christian subjects. In those parts of
the Empire which had been occupied by western Christian
powers any movement for independence and revolt was
naturally directed against them rather than the Porte. In
the spirit of pan-Islam the Egyptian nationalist leader
Mustafa Kamel even supported the Sultan's claim to part of
Sinai in 1904 against Lord Cromer's defence of Egypt's
interests.[3]

The Arab Ottoman provinces were culturally, socially

and economically stagnant. Syria—that is the area which today comprises Lebanon, Syria, Israel and Jordan—was the most advanced but even there cultural life was at a low ebb. Instruction in the few schools that existed was narrowly religious. Books were rare; Arabic newspapers and magazines were unknown. Some of the fine traditional handicrafts survived but there was nothing to compare with the contemporary commercial and industrial expansion of Europe. The Ottoman educational reforms which were introduced towards the end of the nineteenth century brought about some very limited improvement.

Although there was no overt rebellion against the Turks there was an underlying spirit of unrest. Denis de Rivoyre, a Frenchman who travelled extensively in the Arab countries in 1883, reported : 'Everywhere I came upon the same abiding and universal sentiment : hatred of the Turks. The notion of concerted action to throw off the detested yoke is gradually shaping itself. . . . An Arab movement, newly-risen, is looming in the distance; and a race hitherto downtrodden will presently claim its due place in the destinies of Islam. . . .'[4]

But the process was still very gradual. The non-Turkish Muslims, mostly Arabs of the Ottoman Empire, had not as yet evolved any plan to throw off the authority of the Sultan–Caliph in Constantinople. Many of the leaders of this nascent political movement for Arab revival were Christians, but there was no question of their making their own rebellion like the Greeks or the Bulgarians. In the first place they were a too small and scattered minority among Muslims (except in the tiny area of Mount Lebanon) and secondly most of them were Arabs before they were Christians. Whether from design or necessity the Christian Arabs linked their destiny with their Muslim brothers.

The anti-Turkish movement was slow to evolve in the Arab provinces both because of their insulation from the fermenting European ideas of nationalism, and because of the skill and cunning with which Abdul Hamid endeavoured to hold what remained of his Empire together. His method was first to appeal to the religious feelings of his Muslim subjects, while employing every means of intrigue and espionage to detect and counter political opposition or subversion. Only where these appeared to be failing did he make use of outright repression.

Abdul Hamid's immediate predecessors had revived the title of Caliph which had become purely ornamental. Abdul Hamid aimed to carry the process further and to restore the office of Caliph to the position it held in the early days of Islam : the shadow of God on earth and protector of all the Muslim faithful.[5] The principle of the identification of church and state in a single ruler was an integral part of Islam, and Abdul Hamid intended to make use of it. He also aimed to exploit for his own purpose the powerful spirit of pan-Islam engendered by the leading Islamic reformer of the nineteenth century, Jemal al-Din al-Afghani (1839–97), who had preached among the Muslim peoples of many countries the need for them to unite to face the common threat of European expansion. Al-Afghani was prepared to accept the Sultan as Caliph but he certainly did not see the caliphate as an instrument of Ottoman political despotism.[6] After al-Afghani had been deported from Persia by the Shah (he clashed with the authorities in several countries) Abdul Hamid invited him to Istanbul. Although treated with honour al-Afghani ended his days virtually as the Sultan's prisoner.

As we have seen (p. 14) Abdul Hamid's reputation as a liberal and enlightened prince was soon tarnished by his despotic actions, although he remained an active reformer and moderniser in certain important respects. But he took good care that his reputation for piety should be sustained. Where most of his predecessors had been dissolute he was strait-laced and strict in his religious observances. He surrounded himself at his court with scholars and divines, sub-

sidised theological schools and liberally financed Muslim
missionary activities. He made special efforts to win the
hearts of his Arab subjects by pouring money into their
religious institutions and repairing and redecorating their
most historic mosques. He was assisted by the eminent Arab
thinkers he had promoted and honoured.

The crowning achievement of Abdul Hamid's Islamic
policy was the building of the Hejaz Railway from Damascus to the Holy Cities of Mecca and Medina. The project
was master-minded by one of the Sultan's secretaries, Izzat
Pasha al-Abd, a Syrian Arab. It took seven years to build
(1901–8) at a cost of £3 million, of which more than one
third was raised in voluntary donations from all over the
Muslim world. The publicised aim of the project was to
facilitate the transport of Muslim pilgrims to the Holy Cities.
This it did, but at the same time it made it easier to move
troops into the heart of Arabia and thereby strengthened
the Porte's control over the outlying provinces of the Empire.

There was no question of Abdul Hamid's authority as the
Sultan–Caliph resting on his piety alone. Apart from the
divines at his court he promoted a number of Arab administrators such as Izzat Pasha al-Abd, while part of his personal bodyguard consisted of picked Arab recruits. Through
a spider's web of espionage and intrigue radiating from
Constantinople he aimed to detect and deal with any subversive movement in the Arab provinces.

He had a number of picked emissaries scouring the Arab
world in the guise of preachers whose real mission was to
sow or fan discord between feudal chiefs and the heads of
the larger nomadic confederations. Family quarrels, tribal
disputes and blood-feuds were exploited and promoted. He
subsidised agents to provoke disturbances of the peace in
order to provide visible pretexts for the punishment of some
recalcitrant chieftain or leader marked down for vengeance.
He tolerated, and in certain instances ordered, a resort to
assassination. If the victim happened to be too eminent for
summary vengeance, Abdul Hamid would compel him to

reside in Constantinople, and there would not only abstain from having him murdered, but arrange for his living in ease and dignity under the watch of his spies.[7]

The enforced residence in Constantinople of one of the most prominent of these suspects was to have fatal consequences for the Empire. This was Hussein ibn Ali of the Hashemite family of Arabia, which by long tradition had provided the holder of the prestigious Office of Grand Sharif of Mecca. In 1893 Hussein had been politely invited to move to Constantinople and had arrived there with his family. Twenty-three years later it was Hussein who was to raise the flag of the Arab revolt against the Ottoman Turks.

If Abdul Hamid was illiberal and despotic he was no mindless reactionary. He had no intention of becoming a constitutional monarch or allowing the development of representative institutions, but he did see the need for other reforms. Not only the Empire but Turkey's very existence as an independent state was at stake. In the first decade of his reign important reforms were carried through in several fields by his Grand Vezir, Mehmet Said Pasha. Higher education was greatly expanded through the foundation of a score of new schools and colleges, the legal system and court procedure was overhauled (although Said Pasha was unable to do anything to change the Capitulations) and, despite the severe censorship which was a feature of Abdul Hamid's despotism, the circulation of newspapers and journals and the printing of books dealing with religion, language, science, history and the arts increased substantially.

Like some of his predecessors, Abdul Hamid saw the urgent need to improve Turkey's military machine if it was to stand up to the western Powers. For this he was prepared to seek the aid of the rising power of Germany which had recently demonstrated its military strength in the Franco-Prussian war of 1870–71. In 1883 a military mission under Colonel von der Goltz arrived in Constantinople to begin modernising the Ottoman armed forces. His task was not

easy because although Abdul Hamid wanted to improve
the army he did not wish it to become too strong since he
lived in fear of military revolution. He and his ministers
actually intrigued against the mission to prevent it from
being too successful. However, Colonel von der Goltz's
energy and efficiency achieved much in the thirteen years
he spent in Turkey. Abdul Hamid was right to be wary
because one of von der Goltz's biggest successes was to make
the military colleges the best institutions of higher learning
in the country, so that they attracted the most able and
ambitious of his subjects. Eventually, some of these were to
overthrow him.

Despite all these reforms Turkey's relative economic and
military weakness forced Abdul Hamid to use every weapon
of intrigue and diplomacy at his disposal in his relations
with the Powers of Europe. His Islamic policy and his self-
promotion as the Sultan–Caliph were aimed to appeal as
much to the Muslim subjects of other Empires as to his
own : to central Asians ruled by the Russian tsars, to the
Arabs of French North Africa and to Muslims of British
India. He was also able to exploit the rivalries between the
Powers themselves, and the ambitious new power of Kaiser
Wilhelm's Germany provided the obvious balance to the
overweening influence of England and France, the two
countries which had already seized large areas of the Ottoman Empire. Germany was looking eastwards for political
and economic expansion—the policy known as the 'Drang
Nach Osten'. The influx of German capital into Turkey
amounted to an invasion. German companies obtained concessions to extend the railway system of Anatolia, and in
1898 Kaiser Wilhelm II visited Constantinople in person to
secure the concession to carry the line from Konia to
Baghdad. This was the famous Baghdad Railway which
among other things would have created a direct link between the Mediterranean and the Persian Gulf. In addition
to providing immense opportunities to German commercial

enterprise in the Near East it offered a direct strategic threat to the British position in India.

The invitation to the German military mission had grown into a Turco-German axis. Kaiser Wilhelm continued his tour from Constantinople to Jerusalem and Damascus, stressing at all times his sympathies for Islam and the Sultan–Caliph. In Damascus he said : 'His Majesty the Sultan and the three hundred million Moslems who revere him as the Caliph may rest assured that they will always have a friend in the German Emperor.' The majority of the three hundred million were not subjects of the Sultan but of Germany's rivals.

Neither Abdul Hamid's diplomatic skill nor his elaborate precautions against subversion could prevent the growth of opposition to his despotism. From 1889 onwards the Young Turk movement, as it was called, continuously gathered support especially among students at the military colleges. At this stage they were not highly organised, although they maintained links with various groups of exiles in Paris, Cairo and elsewhere, who were publishing newspapers and journals attacking the Sultan. In 1895 a clandestine organisation of Young Turks in Constantinople adopted the name of Committee of Union and Progress. An attempted coup in 1896 was crushed and its leaders exiled, but the movement continued to grow. Abdul Hamid tried to win over the exiles with a mixture of threats and promises, but they resisted and in 1899 were joined by one of his own cousins. In 1906 there was a development which was ultimately fatal to Abdul Hamid when revolutionary cells began to be formed by serving officers in the field. The first, which included the young Mustafa Kemal, was in Damascus, but the most important was among the officers of the Third Army Corps in Salonika.

Events now moved rapidly. The cadets had by now become captains and majors, with men and arms under their command; the parlous state of the armed forces, and the increasing dangers of secession and aggression, made a change of régime an urgent necessity obvious to any patriotic and aspiring young officer. These were not of the kind that was to be familiar in subsequent Middle East revolutions— ambitious young subalterns, drawn from new and rising social classes, using the discipline and cohesion of the army to destroy an old social order and initiate a revolutionary upheaval. They were members of a ruling *élite*, prepared by education to command and to govern; their complaint was that they were not permitted to do so effectively. The army, mistrusted by the Sultan, was starved of money and equipment, its pay in arrears and its weapons obsolete. Smart young officers, with up-to-date training for an out-of-date army, could not but be painfully aware of the inadequacy of the defences of the Empire, in the face of the dangers that were looming. Their political ideas were simple and rudimentary—freedom and fatherland, the constitution and the nation.[8]

In the summer of 1908 matters came to a head when the rumbling discontent throughout the armed forces in Turkey turned into open mutiny, which spread from the Third Army Corps in Macedonia to the Second Army Corps in Edirne. The Committee of Union and Progress (C.U.P.) then came into the open and formalised the aims of the mutineers in a demand for the restoration of the Midhat Constitution of 1876. Abdul Hamid hesitated and then, on 24 July, gave way. On the following day he released all political prisoners, abolished the censorship and disbanded his corps of 30,000 spies.

The success of the Young Turks' revolution raised high hopes throughout the Empire and beyond. It was greeted as the beginning of a new era of liberty and constitutional government, and Turks and non-Turks in the Empire shared in the rejoicing. However, it soon became apparent that the various elements who made up the Empire held widely differing views of the kind of political system which should replace Abdul Hamid's despotism. In particular there were two contrasting, and ultimately incompatible, ideologies :

Turkish nationalism and Ottoman liberalism. The former meant the continuation and strengthening of the domination of the Turkish race, language and culture, while the latter implied the principle of equality for all the Turkish and non-Turkish, Muslim and non-Muslim elements within the Empire. Ottoman liberalism was the underlying principle of Midhat's constitution, if somewhat naïvely and idealistically expressed, but the leaders of the Young Turks were overwhelmingly Turkish nationalist in outlook. They used their newly-won power to interpret the constitution in accordance with their ideas. There were liberal elements among the revolutionaries, but they were weak and divided and no match for the vigorous and decisive Turkish nationalists.

No reliable statistics exist, but the population of the Ottoman Empire in 1908 (excluding Egypt) was approximately 22 million of whom 7·5 million were Turks, 10·5 million Arab and the remaining 4 million Greeks, Albanians, Armenians, Kurds and smaller communities. The Turks were therefore outnumbered by Arabs by about two to one.[9] By the selection of candidates and the demarcation of constituencies for the elections held under the revised constitution, the C.U.P. ensured that 150 Turks and 60 Arabs were elected out of a total of 245 members of the Chamber of Deputies. Among the 40 members of the Senate appointed by the Sultan only three were Arabs.

As we have seen, the simmering hatred of the Turks among the Arabs had not led to any open revolt against Abdul Hamid. A secret society founded in Beirut, mainly by Christian Arabs, had drafted an independence programme for the Arab provinces and called for an uprising. The Arab nationalist writings of Abdul-Rahman al-Kawakabi (1849-1903), a Syrian Arab who found refuge from Ottoman censorship in Egypt, attracted some interest. But Abdul Hamid's police system was too ruthless and efficient for the infant Arab national movement to grow, while his pan-Islamic policies were at least partially successful in dampening the spirit of revolt among Muslim Arabs. The spirit of Egyptian nationalism was growing, but it was directed primarily against the British occupiers. At this period it had almost no connection with the Arab national movement.

The Arabs' reaction to the Young Turks' revolution was initially enthusiastic. They were not an important element in the C.U.P.; 'although a few Arabs, most of them army officers, had joined the party and worked hand-in-glove with its leaders, they had done so as Ottoman citizens rather than as Arab nationalists.'[10] In fact Ottoman Jews occupied a more important place than the Arabs in the movement. Nevertheless, the Arabs could support the common aim of overthrowing the Hamidian despotism and hope that it would lead to genuine equality between the races of the Empire. Shortly after the coup a new society called the Ottoman Arab Fraternity (al-Ikha' al-Arabi al-Uthmani) was founded at a big meeting of the Arab community in Constantinople attended by the C.U.P. leaders. As a gesture of goodwill the C.U.P. decided to end the sixteen years' exile of the Sharif Hussein ibn Ali and send him back to Arabia as the Grand Sharif of Mecca. They ignored the cautionary advice of Abdul Hamid; in this matter he proved wiser than they.

'Constitutionalism' was the watchword of the day. Japan's victory over Russia in 1905 had had a tremendous impact throughout the Muslim world not only because it was the first example for several centuries of a supposedly backward Asian state defeating one of the Christian Powers of Europe, but also of a constitutional government proving more efficient than an autocracy. The Young Turks sincerely hoped that their constitution would do the same for them, but because they looked upon it as a means of restoring and strengthening Turkish power they soon disappointed the hopes of the non-Turks in the Empire.

The Turkish-Arab honeymoon was short-lived. The results of the Ottoman parliamentary elections had already revealed the Young Turks' intention of keeping real power in the Empire firmly in Turkish hands when an event occurred which caused them to intensify their authoritarian attitudes. In April 1909 Abdul Hamid attempted a counter-revolution by inciting the Constantinople garrison to mutiny against the C.U.P. After an initial success the revolt was suppressed and Abdul Hamid was deposed. The Young Turks replaced him with his colourless brother Prince Reshad who took the name Mohammed V. He could be relied upon not to interfere with the Young Turks' authority. One of their first acts was to ban the Ottoman Arab Fraternity and the other societies formed by non-Turkish minorities within the empire.

In fact the circumstances could hardly have been less auspicious for a liberalisation of the Empire, since it was threatened on all sides by the Christian powers of Europe. In their first four years of power the Young Turks lost all the remaining European provinces in Europe (except for eastern Thrace). Austria–Hungary annexed Bosnia and Herzegovina in 1908, Bulgaria finally seceded to become independent, Italy invaded Libya and seized the provinces of Tripoli and Benghazi, and Greece took Crete and the Dodecanese. In reaction to these disasters the Young Turks were strongly influenced by pan-Turanian or Turkish irredentist ideas, that is to say the notion that all the Turkish-speaking Muslim peoples of Anatolia and central Asia formed a single nation. Clearly this was incompatible with any doctrine of Arab-Turkish equality. But the other strain of thinking which influenced the Young Turks—Ottomanism or the strengthening of the multi-racial empire—was not only inconsistent with pan-Turanism, but equally inimical to Arab aspirations because it aimed at the fusion of the different races in a single centralised Ottoman system with Turkish as its distinctive language.

Arab agitation for reform did not cease, but it was forced either to go underground or to act with great caution. In Constantinople the important Arab Literary Club was formed in 1909. It could escape suppression only as long as it remained non-political, but it exerted considerable indirect political influence. In 1912 the Ottoman Decentralisation Party was founded in Cairo, where British protection ensured its relative freedom of action, with the object of impressing both the rulers of the Empire and Arab public opinion with the need for administrative decentralisation. In addition several Arab secret societies were formed of which the two most important were *al-Qahtaniya,* led by Major Aziz Ali al-Masri (later Inspector-General of the Egyptian Army), and *al-Fatat* or the Young Arab Society, which was founded in Paris in 1911. Al-Qahtaniya aimed to unite the Ottoman Arab provinces in a single kingdom within the Empire, which would then become a Turco-Arab dual monarchy along the lines of the Austro-Hungarian Empire. Al-Fatat, the most important of all these societies, aimed at complete independence for the Arab provinces. It moved its headquarters from Paris to Beirut and then to Damascus where its membership rapidly increased.

Early in 1913 a group of prominent Arabs who had formed themselves into a Committee of Reform in Beirut published concrete proposals for reform which, while accepting the authority of Constantinople (as they had to do if they were to avoid immediate suppression), advocated devolution of regional administration to representative local bodies, the adoption of Arabic as a language on an equal footing with Turkish in the Ottoman parliament and the ending of the practice of conscripting soldiers for service outside their own provinces. When this move aroused a widespread response throughout Syria and Iraq the C.U.P. dissolved the Committee of Reform and closed its headquarters.

On the initiative of al-Fatat the movement then shifted to

Paris, where an Arab national congress was held in June 1913. The meeting was hastily organised, and the overwhelming majority of the delegates came from Syria rather than the other Arab provinces of the Empire. However, it aroused considerable international interest and caused the C.U.P. to react. Having failed to persuade the French to ban the congress, they sent their secretary to Paris to enter into negotiations with its leaders. The agreement that they reached appeared to be an important victory for the Arabs. Arabic became the official language in the Arab provinces and the medium of instruction in primary and secondary schools, and the important point about localising military service was conceded. There were to be five Arab governors-general and a minimum of three Arab ministers in the Ottoman government. But once again Arab hopes were rapidly disappointed as it soon became clear that the C.U.P. had no intention of fulfilling their promises. The concessions were either whittled down until they had no substance or their application was indefinitely postponed. By the beginning of 1914 the great majority of leading Arabs had abandoned all hopes of reaching an accommodation with the C.U.P. In February 1914 anti-Turkish feeling among the Arabs hardened with the arrest and trial of the founder of al-Qahtaniya, Major Aziz al-Masri. He had replaced al-Qahtaniya with a new society, al-Ahd (the Covenant), which consisted almost entirely of army officers, with a preponderance of Iraqis, who were the most numerous Arab element in the Ottoman Army. The C.U.P. may well have known about al-Ahd but they preferred to accuse al-Masri of other more heinous, if less probable, crimes, such as selling Cyrenaica to the Italians. When it became known that al-Masri had been secretly condemned to death the public outcry was reinforced by a strong British protest. Eventually al-Masri was released and allowed to return to Egypt.

The year that was to be fatal for the Ottoman Empire thus saw a sharp deterioration in relations between its two main elements—the Turks and the Arabs. But Ottoman power in the remaining provinces was not noticeably in decline. Despite the occasional strikes and disturbances in favour of reform Turkish rule in Syria and Iraq was firm. The Hejaz Railway had helped to consolidate the Turkish hold in eastern Arabia although the Grand Sharif Hussein, appointed by the C.U.P., was already giving them cause to remember the warnings of the ex-Sultan, Abdul Hamid, against him. In the more remote parts of the Arabian peninsula Ottoman authority had always been light. In the Yemen a compromise had been reached in 1911 with the Imam Yahya whereby the latter, in return for acceptance of Turkish suzerainty, acquired virtual independence in the mountainous interior, while the Turks remained in control of the Red Sea Tihama plain. A similar arrangement had been made with Muhammad Ibn Ali al-Idrisi, ruler of Asir, the province immediately to the north of the Tihama. In central Arabia the young Abdul Aziz Ibn Saud, who had ousted his rival Shaikh Rashid from the Nejd in 1904, had gone on to seize the west Arabian province of al-Hasa from the Turks in 1913. But this Turkish reverse was balanced by the close relations established with the Rashidi tribes who remained in control of the Shammar region of northern Arabia. British influence in Arabia, which had begun to be established in the first half of the nineteenth century, had been consolidated, but remained confined to the southern and eastern periphery of the peninsula.

When the first Arab National Congress had been held in Paris in 1913, its sponsors had claimed that one of the chief reasons for holding the meeting was that Ottoman denial of Arab aspirations was threatening the Arab provinces with chaos and increasing the danger of foreign intervention. 'Foreign' meant 'European', and in order to avoid offending the French authorities the matter had to be handled tactfully at the Congress. But it was always foremost in the minds of the delegates and it is easy to understand why. In

the entire Muslim world, outside what was left of the Ottoman Empire, European influence and control had grown
stronger. Egypt, after a short period of quasi-liberalisation
during the consul-generalship of Eldon Gorst (who succeeded
Lord Cromer in 1907), was in the masterful grip of Lord
Kitchener. Libya, with the exception of the Cyrenaican
plateau, was under Italian occupation, while the ancient
kingdom of Morocco had finally been partitioned into
French and Spanish Protectorates in 1908. Even Persia, the
former great rival of the Ottoman Empire, was not immune
from European encroachment. It was principally the subject
of the ambitions of its northern neighbour Russia, and of
Britain, concerned as always to protect its imperial communications with India. In 1907 an Anglo-Russian agreement had virtually partitioned the whole country into
spheres of influence for the two Powers. A further reason
for British interest in Persia was the decision which was
taken in principle in 1904 by the Admiralty to convert the
Royal Navy from the use of coal to oil as fuel. In 1908 oil
was struck in southern Persia by the Anglo-Persian Oil
Company in the first major oil field to be discovered in the
Middle East.

Nevertheless it was Turkey that remained the dominating
power in the Arab heartlands, and it was against Turkey
that the Arab national movement in the twentieth century
was first directed. Moreover, the leading Arabs in the Ottoman provinces were prepared to seek the help of the European powers—notably Britain—in their efforts to overthrow
Turkish domination. In the spring of 1914 Sharif Hussein of
Mecca's second son, Amir Abdullah, made tentative ap-
proaches to Lord Kitchener, the British Agent and Consul
General in Egypt, to sound out Britain's attitude in the
event of the occurrence of an open conflict between Turks
and Arabs. The Sharif was aware that the C.U.P. intended
to depose him and he knew that this was likely to lead to an
open revolt in the Hejaz. Kitchener's reply was extremely

cautious. Britain's policy of sustaining Turkey as a bulwark against Russian expansionism had not been finally abandoned however feeble the Sick Man of Europe might have become. However, the conversation and later discussions between the Amir Abdullah and Ronald Storrs, Kitchener's Oriental Secretary, helped to convince Kitchener of the depth of Arab animosity towards the Turks.[11] This shaped Britain's policy towards the Arabs when she finally broke with Turkey.

The division between Arabs and Turks was essentially a family dispute between relatives. This did not make it any less bitter, but the separation did not destroy at one blow the close affinity derived from centuries of symbiosis in an Islamic community in which racial 'apartheid' was unknown. In principle the governors, senior administrators and judges in the Ottoman Empire's provinces were sent from Constantinople and appointed for one year only to prevent them from putting down roots and identifying themselves with the local community. In practice—especially in the more outlying areas of the Empire—a large share of political power passed into the hands of the local élite of sheikhs, *ulema* and landowners, and this was accepted by the Sultan's government in Constantinople. The ruling groups in the various provinces as well as Turkey proper together constituted a real entity : the Ottoman governing class. This may have varied in composition from one part of the Empire to another—a Berber element in North Africa, Circassian in Egypt, Kurdish in Iraq—but it had certain common characteristics. Its members mingled freely and frequently intermarried. In the nineteenth century, when the Sultan's Arab provinces were reduced to Syria, Iraq and parts of Arabia, they shared a common education in the secondary schools and colleges which had been created by the Ottoman educational reforms. Only a few of the Arab Ottoman élite were educated at the foreign institutions of learning in Cairo or Beirut.

Initially the Arab antagonism towards Turkish rule was more cultural than political or administrative in origin. The Arabs deeply resented the 'Turkification' of the educational system and the replacement of Arabic by Turkish for all except religious studies. After the bitterness engendered by the Arab struggle for independence, Arab writers and historians tended to understimate the value of Ottoman educational reforms, which began with the education law of 1869 providing in theory for a minimum compulsory schooling of four years from the age of seven. In 1914 there were some 400 state schools in Syria with some 21,000 pupils at the elementary level and about 900 at the secondary and higher levels. In Iraq there were about 170 schools of all grades with about 7400 elementary and 1200 secondary and high school pupils.[12] These numbers may appear miserably inadequate, but it was to be some years before they were improved upon after the overthrow of Ottoman rule. Moreover, the Arabs soon became aware that 'While the Turks laid no claim to a superiority over the Arabs in civilisation, the Europeans did so with undisguised arrogance. For in their different ways the British, the French and even the Italians and Spaniards took it for granted that they had special insight into what was in the best interests of their Arab subjects, and accordingly rejected or sidetracked Arab attempts at improving their educational lot.'[13]

3 The End of Empire 1914-1920

WHEN war broke out in the summer of 1914 between the Allies (Britain, France and Russia) and the Central Powers (Germany and Austro-Hungary) it was by no means a foregone conclusion that Turkey would side with the latter. Turkey was effectively ruled by a triumvirate of Young Turks—Enver, Talaat and Jemal. While they were alarmed by Russia's long-standing ambitions towards Constantinople they were also concerned with German imperial expansionism. A British naval mission headed by Admiral Limpus was liked and trusted, while the British Ambassador, Sir Louis Mallet, had established excellent relations with the Porte. Ultimately, however, the matter was decided in favour of the Central Powers because Enver Pasha, who was the dominant figure in the Ottoman government, was inclined towards Germany. On 2 August 1914 the Germans succeeded in concluding a secret alliance with Turkey in Constantinople, and on 5 November Turkey declared war on the Allies (see Ann Williams *Britain and France in the Middle East and North Africa*, pp. 9-10).

This fatal decision was to affect the political status of the peoples of the central Islamic countries for several generations. If Germany had won the war the Ottoman Empire and caliphate might have survived, although the Empire could hardly have escaped radical transformation. The Bolshevik Revolution of 1917, by eliminating Russia from the war, almost certainly saved Turkey from losing Constantinople and some of its northern provinces, but the Anglo-French victory in the war ensured that European

Christian hegemony spread to nearly all the Muslim areas which had hitherto escaped it.

The Ottoman Empire was a more formidable enemy than the Allies had generally supposed. The reforms instituted by Abdul Hamid and continued by the Young Turks had produced some results. The Allies' attempt to knock Turkey out of the war in 1915, through the Dardanelles expedition, was a costly failure. The Turks retained the fighting qualities which had terrified Christendom four centuries earlier. Ultimately these were no match for the overwhelming technical and organisational superiority of the Allies— although they did ensure that the Turkish heartland of Anatolia was preserved from dismemberment when the war was over. But the weakness of the Ottoman Empire as a whole was the animosity between Turks and the majority of its subjects, the Arabs. It was this weakness that the Allies were ready and eager to exploit.

In 1914 the Allies were less concerned with Turkey's military power than the effect that going to war with the world's principal Islamic state and its Sultan–Caliph might have on their own millions of Muslim subjects in French North-west Africa, in British India and in Russian central Asia. In Europe it had been the custom for many generations to equate 'Muhammadans' (as they were usually, if incorrectly, called*) with 'fanaticism', and it was popularly supposed that any true Muslim was only waiting for a suitable opportunity to slaughter the infidel. 'Jihad', or Holy War, had after all been enjoined upon the Muslim Faithful as a sacred duty by the Prophet Muhammad, and inevitably the C.U.P. lost no time in calling upon all true believers to rise against their European rulers. Britain was especially concerned, both because of the large numbers of Muslims in the Indian Army and because of its strategically vital position

---

* Because Muslims worship the one God and not his Prophet Muhammad, in their eyes the use of the term 'Muhammadan' is equivalent to calling Christians 'Paulines'.

in Egypt, where the population was not only predominantly Muslim, but many of the upper class of beys and pashas were Turkish by race and outlook. As things turned out, British fears were exaggerated. There was little public expression of pan-Islamic feeling among the Egyptian public and it scarcely affected the armed forces. Some Muslim troops in two Indian battalions of the Suez Canal Defence Force deserted to the Turks; those who were caught were shot and the trouble was prevented from spreading. A succession of Indian Muslim ruling princes visited the Canal zone to help stiffen the morale of the troops. Soon after war with Turkey was declared Britain ended the nominal Ottoman suzerainty over Egypt, which became a British Protectorate, and replaced the pro-Turkish Khedive (that is to say, hereditary Viceroy) Abbas II with his elderly uncle, Hussein Kamel, who was given the title of Sultan. All this took place with virtually no public opposition inside Egypt. It merely gave formed expression to the fact of British control over Egypt, which had lasted for three decades.

If the Sultan–Caliph's call to Jihad was finally only of minor concern to the Allies it placed the Grand Sharif of Mecca in an awkward position. Before the outbreak of war, when it was far from inevitable that Turkey would be drawn into it, Sharif Hussein had been prepared for a struggle with Constantinople to assert his independent rights in the Hejaz. Turkey's entry into the war gave him two choices : either he could answer the call to Jihad by siding with Turkey and hope that after the war the grateful Turks would satisfy Arab aspirations, or he could throw in his lot with the Allies in the hope that they would help the Arabs to win their own independence. The choice was appallingly difficult because it depended on so many unforeseeable factors. His own family was divided, with Amir Abdullah favouring an alliance with Britain and his younger son Feisal (later king of Syria and Iraq) at that time inclined towards siding with Turkey.

In either case, a decision could not long be delayed as Turkish demands for a response to the appeal for Jihad became more insistent. Nevertheless the Sharif managed to stall them skilfully for several months. Meanwhile he was continuously sounding out Britain to see what guarantees of support for the Arab national movement he could expect if he were to take the risky step of raising a revolt against the Turks and sending emissaries into Syria, Iraq and elsewhere in Arabia to test the reactions of the Arabs in these areas.

Kitchener, at Ronald Storrs's suggestion, had approached the Sharif Hussein six weeks before Turkey entered the war to find out which way the Arabs would turn if Turkey allied itself to Germany. The Sharif had been as cautious as Kitchener himself had been with Amir Abdullah eight months earlier. Carefully confining his remarks to the areas under his jurisdiction (that is excluding Syria, Iraq, the Nejd or Yemen), he hinted that he might bring the Hejazis out in revolt against the Turks if he was ensured of enough British support. A further message from Kitchener (who by now was Minister of War in the British Cabinet) promised Hussein that if he would come out against Turkey Britain would guarantee his retention of the title of Grand Sharif and defend him against external aggression. It hinted that if the Sharif was declared Caliph he would have Britain's support, and included a general promise to help the Arabs obtain their freedom.[1]

This message was enough to cause the Sharif Hussein to contemplate the much wider objective of a general Arab revolt against the Turks under his leadership. But for this he required much more specific assurances from the Allies, and the year 1915 was spent trying to elicit them from Cairo while he continued to sound out the opinion of the other leading Arabs with whom he was in contact. In Arabia Ibn Rashid of the Shammar region and the Imam Yahya were pro-Turk, while Ibn Saud in the Nejd, al-Idrisi in Asir and the Ruler of Kuwait (which was linked to Britain by the treaty of alliance of 1899) were anti-Turk, although they were unable to offer any positive contribution to an Arab revolt. Ibn Saud had been compelled to accept the overlord-ship of the Sultan in 1914, but he now threw this off and in December 1915 signed a treaty with the British government which gave Britain a large measure of control over his foreign policy, but acknowledged the independence and territorial integrity of the Nejd and granted him an annual subsidy.[2] An emissary from al-Fatat in Syria assured the Sharif of support from that quarter, but Syria was under the iron grip of Jemal Pasha, the leading member of the C.U.P. who had been appointed Governor and Com-mander-in-Chief of the Ottoman forces in Syria.

Meanwhile the British for their part were trying to make up their minds how far they should go in responding to the Sharif Hussain's demands. With his unique position in the Islamic world and his relatively independent status, the Sharif was not only the obvious person to lead an Arab revolt against the Turks, but the one who could most effec-tively counter the effect of the call to Jihad. But at that stage Britain had almost no knowledge of the state of opinion inside Syria and Iraq, although she was in a position to sound the feelings of leading Arabs in Cairo. Moreover she had to consider the interests of her principal allies, Russia and France, especially the latter whose claim to a special position in Syria, based on long-standing cultural and political ties, had been acknowledged by Britain before the war. The government of India also, which, though British, had its own interests and means of pressure in Whitehall, regarded the Arabian peninsula as its special concern. It had been responsible for negotiating the treaty with Ibn Saud.

The negotiations between Britain and the Sharif and the agreement which led to his final decision to raise the flag of revolt against the Turks are embodied in an exchange of letters known as the Hussein–McMahon correspondence.

Sir Henry McMahon, the British High Commissioner in Egypt, was delegated to act in this matter on the British government's behalf.

The correspondence took place between July 1915 and February 1916. After the war Sir Henry McMahon's letters were to be the basis of Arab nationalist charges against Britain of betrayal.[3] Others have denied that any breach of faith was involved, on the ground that the Sharif Hussein must have known of the existence of separate Anglo-French negotiations on the future of the Arab provinces of the Ottoman Empire and of their real intentions towards them.[4] But regardless of whether the Sharif must or should have been aware of Britain's plans, there can be no doubt that they were incompatible with some of the pledges contained in McMahon's letters.

The Sharif's aim was to elicit British support for Arab independence in all the Arab provinces of the Ottoman Empire from Mersin in the north, the Persian frontier in the east, the Mediterranean in the west and the Red Sea and Indian Ocean in the south. The only temporary exception he was prepared to make was Aden. No doubt he was aware that Britain would not agree to all this, but, like most negotiators, he began with his maximum bargaining position. The crucial McMahon letter is his second, dated 24 October 1915, in which he pledged British support for Arab independence in the areas requested by the Sharif with the following reservations :

The districts of Mersin and Alexandretta, and portions of Syria lying to the west of the districts of Damascus, Homs, Hama and Aleppo, cannot be said to be purely Arab, and must on that account be excepted from the proposed delimitation.

Subject to that modification, and without prejudice to the treaties concluded between us and certain Arab Chiefs, we accept that delimitation.

As for the regions lying within the proposed frontiers, in which Great Britain is free to act without detriment to the interests of her ally France, I am authorised to give you the following pledges on behalf of the Government of Great Britain, and to reply as follows to your note :

That subject to the modifications stated above, Great Britain is prepared to recognise and uphold the independence of the Arabs in all the regions lying within the frontiers proposed by the Sharif of Mecca.

Two other passages in this letter are worth noting :

That it is understood that the Arabs have already decided to seek the counsels and advice of Great Britain exclusively; and that such European advisers and officials as may be needed to establish a sound system of administration shall be British :

That, as regards to the two Vilayets of Baghdad and Basra the Arabs recognise that the fact of Great Britain's established position and interests there will call for the setting up of special administrative arrangements to protect those regions from foreign aggression, to promote the welfare of their inhabitants and to safeguard our mutual interests.*

There is considerable ambiguity about the key phrases in this letter, and this ambiguity was no doubt deliberate. The British government was by now extremely anxious to have the Sharif as an ally, but it did not want to arouse French suspicions of its intentions, and it had not made up its mind whether to deal with the Sharif as the acknowledged leader of all the Arabs or only of those of the Hejaz.[5] The phrase 'portions of Syria lying to the west of the districts of Damascus, Homs, Hama and Aleppo' presumably refers to an area roughly corresponding to Lebanon of the present day and the Mediterranean coastal area of Syria. It could not be said to have included Palestine. It could be argued that Palestine was not mentioned in any of the correspondence because Palestine was not an Ottoman administrative division, although it was a geographical expression employed throughout the Christian world. But by no stretch of the

* The British had landed troops at Basra in 1914 and were trying to take Iraq (Mesopotamia) from the Turks.

imagination could McMahon's pledge be said to have excluded from the area of Arab independence either the Sanjak of Jerusalem (the southern half of Palestine) or the greater part of Syria. It may be that the Sharif was aware that Palestine was implicitly excluded but there is no proof of this assertion and the most obvious interpretation of McMahon's second letter is that it was not excluded.

In his reply to McMahon's second letter the Sharif accepted the modification excluding Mersin and Adana (now part of Turkey) from the Arab kingdom, but refused to consider the 'Vilayets of Aleppo and Beirut and their western maritime coasts' as anything but Arab provinces. On the question of the Iraqi provinces he compromised, pointing out that because they were part of the former Arab Empire, the seat of the caliphs and the first centre of Arab culture it would be 'impossible to persuade or compel the Arab nation to renounce the honourable association'; he agreed that for the sake of British interests those areas at that time occupied by British troops (mainly the province of Basra) should 'remain so occupied for a period to be determined by negotiation, without prejudice to the rights of either party or the natural wealth and resources of these parts'.

In a further letter McMahon wrote that the British government had understood and carefully noted the Sharif's statement concerning the two Vilayets of Aleppo and Beirut, 'but as the interests of their ally France are involved in these two provinces, the question calls for careful consideration'.

In his reply to this the Sharif declared his willingness to shelve the question in the interests of avoiding anything which might possibly injure the alliance of Britain and France but that 'at the first opportunity after the war is finished, we shall ask you (what we avert our eyes from today) for what we now leave to France in Beirut and its coasts'.

It is clear that the Sharif was placing considerable trust

in Britain to defend the interests of the Arabs when the war
was over. He was no doubt aware that Britain, with its
military base in Egypt, was certain to emerge from the war
as a stronger power than France in the area and he had
confidence in British integrity. At the same time he was
anxious to wind up the negotiations, which had now lasted
for over a year, so that the Arab Revolt could begin. His
means of warding off Turkish suspicions were becoming
exhausted, while the situation was bringing matters to a
head.

Jemal Pasha's first policy in Syria had been to try to
secure the whole-hearted support of the Muslim majority
of the population for the Turkish war effort. But after the
failure of his first attempts to invade Egypt across the Suez
Canal his intelligence services made him aware of the great
scale of underground Arab anti-Turkish activities. He resorted to a policy of repression. First he took every opportunity to send Arab units of the Ottoman Army out of Syria
and replace them with Turks, and then he put on trial before
a military court a number of prominent Arab civilians who
had been implicated in treasonable activities by documents
seized in the French consulates. Eleven were publicly exe-
cuted in August 1915 and twenty-one more the following
January.[6]

The Sharif knew that he had to act, especially as a large
Turco-German force was about to arrive in the Hejaz on its
way to Yemen. After recalling his son Feisal from Damascus,
where he had been urgently summoned by Jemal Pasha,
Hussein raised the flag of the Arab Revolt on 10 June 1916
and seized Mecca from its small Turkish garrison. The
Sharif had hoped for a landing of Allied troops at Alexandretta to facilitate a simultaneous uprising against the Turks
in Syria, but, although this plan was vigorously supported
by the British military commanders in the Near East, it was
turned down by the British war cabinet, partly because of
French opposition to any landing in Syria with other than

French troops. The Turks held Syria too firmly for an upris-
ing to take place without external support so the Arab
Revolt remained confined to the Hejaz until the allied
advance from Egypt the following year. On 2 November
1916 the Sharif Hussein was proclaimed 'King of the Arab
Countries' by his followers, but this was not acceptable to
Britain and France. A compromise was reached, and in
January 1917 they both recognised him as King of the
Hejaz.

The immediate effect of the Revolt in the Arabian peninsula was considerable. Ibn Rashid and the Imam of Yemen
remained pro-Turkish but they were now isolated, and at
a meeting in Kuwait in November Ibn Saud, the Ruler of
Kuwait, and a number of minor chieftains, declared their
open support for England and the Arabs. But in Iraq there
was no response to the Revolt for several reasons. Like Syria
it was under firm Turkish control, and most of the potential
Arab leaders were serving away from home in the Ottoman
army. But it was equally important that Iraq was regarded
as the concern of the government of India, which never
looked favourably on the Sharifian revolt. Indian Muslims,
who formed a vital element in the Indian army, were deeply
attached to the Caliphate and had no regard for Arab
nationalism.

As it was, the Arab revolt immobilised some 30,000
Turkish troops along the railway from Amman to Medina,
and prevented the Turco-German forces in Syria from link-
ing up with the Turkish garrison in Yemen. There could have
been the most serious consequences for the Allies if the enemy
forces in Arabia had made contact with the Germans in
East Africa and succeeded in closing the Red Sea to Allied
shipping. Arab forces, who were mainly armed tribesmen
with a core of regular troops, carried out valuable guerrilla
operations on the right flank of the British Expeditionary
Force from Egypt as it advanced into Palestine. By a daring
stroke they captured Aqaba in July 1917. These operations

would not have been possible without the help of the British navy on the Hejaz coast, and the co-operation of several British officers, of whom T. E. Lawrence is only the best known. The Arabs made an important contribution to the defeat of the Turks, but there was little they could do on their own.

The burden of the Arab charge of betrayal rests on the fact that when the Revolt began Britain had already entered into a secret agreement with France and Russia on the partition of the Ottoman Empire, in which Britain was less than frank with its other two partners about the pledges made to the Arabs during 1915. The accord is known as the Sykes–Picot Agreement[7] after the principal French and British negotiators, Georges Picot and Sir Mark Sykes. According to the Agreement the whole of Syria and Iraq and a large area of southern Turkey were to be partitioned into spheres of direct or indirect French and British influence. In the so-called 'red' and 'blue' areas Britain and France would be 'allowed to establish such direct or indirect administration or control' as they desired. The British red area comprised most of the Ottoman Vilayets of Baghdad and Basra as well as the ports of Haifa and Acre on the coast of Palestine. The French blue area covered the coast of Syria including Alexandretta, Latakia, Tripoli, Beirut, Tyre and Sidon, and included a large area of central and southern Asia Minor. In addition there were the 'A' and 'B' areas in which France and Britain were prepared 'to recognise and uphold an independent Arab state or a confederation of Arab states' under the suzerainty of an Arab chief. France's 'A' area comprised Mosul and all the principal towns of Syria—Damascus, Aleppo, Homs and Hama. Britain's 'B' area stretched from Kirkuk to Amman and was mainly desert. In addition there was an area coloured brown on the map, covering Jerusalem and part of Palestine, which was to be under some form of international organisation.

As we have seen, the Sharif Hussein must have had more

than an inkling of Britain and France's real intentions towards Syria and Iraq. His apprehensions grew in the early months of 1917, and in May Sir Mark Sykes was sent to Jedda by the British Foreign Office to allay his fears. But although Sykes and Hussein discussed the question of French aims in Lebanon and on the Syrian coast, with Hussein maintaining the principle that these were as much Arab in character as the interior, Sykes did not inform him of the details of the broader aspects of the Sykes–Picot agreement.[8] He only learned of these in November 1917, when the Bolsheviks had seized power in Russia and discovered documents referring to the Sykes–Picot agreement among the imperial archives. They informed the Turks, who lost no time in passing them on to the Arabs as proof of treachery against the Muslim peoples of the Ottoman Empire on the part of the Christian Powers.

The revelation was clearly embarrassing to Britain. Hussein at once asked for an explanation from Sir Reginald Wingate (who had succeeded McMahon in Cairo). Wingate represented the Petrograd documents as referring to provisional exchanges between the British, French and Russian governments rather than any hard agreement, and suggested that the success of the Arab Revolt and the withdrawal of Russia from the war had created an entirely new situation. This was true as far as it went but the 'new situation' did not mean that the prospects for Arab independence had improved. Under Allenby's brilliant generalship the Allied forces had advanced into Palestine to take Jerusalem on 9 December. He was held up by the severe winter and the stiffening of Turco-German resistance, but in September 1918 he resumed his advance to drive the Turks out of Syria. Damascus fell on 1 October, Beirut on 8 October and Aleppo on 26 October. The advance halted on 30 October when Turkey capitulated by signing the Mudros Armistice : the Ottoman Empire, which had lasted four hundred years, came to an end.[9]

Wild Arab rejoicing greeted the liberation of Syria. The civil population had suffered fearfully from the war, because a plague of locusts, combined with the normal disruption of war and the corruption of Turkish officials and Syrian merchants, had caused widespread famine. Between one third and half a million people died out of a total population of four million.[10]

It was Allenby's policy wherever possible to allow Feisal's troops to enter the captured cities triumphantly and take over the administration. But the entente with France was clearly Britain's first consideration, and when France objected to the display of Feisal's flag in Beirut Allenby ordered its removal. The *de facto* application of the Sykes–Picot Agreement had already begun. Iraq was placed under a single Anglo-Indian administration with a British civil commissioner at its head. The British Occupied Enemy Territory Administration South (O.E.T.A. South) covered approximately the area of the subsequent Palestinian mandate, and the French O.E.T.A. East covered the Syrian interior. The French-administered O.E.T.A. West comprised the whole Syrian and Lebanon coastal area from Tyre to Cilicia.

Nevertheless, the Allies had taken steps to try to allay Arab fears. In the spring of 1918 a group of seven prominent Arabs living in Cairo had presented a memorandum asking for a clear definition of British policy. The British reply, which became known as the Declaration to the Seven,[11] was given the widest publicity. Referring to the Arab territories liberated by the actions of the Arab armies, the British government declared its policy in these to be that 'the future government of those territories should be based upon the principle of the consent of the governed'. With regard to those territories still under Turkish rule (that is most of Syria and northern Iraq) the British government merely asserted its desire 'that the oppressed peoples in these territories should obtain their freedom and independence'.

The phrase referring to the 'consent of the governed' in the third category is particularly significant because it was at least nominally the basis of the post-war settlement. It was given immense moral force by its inclusion in July among the 'Four Ends' of peace of the American President, Woodrow Wilson, which were to be embodied in the League of Nations Covenant. It was further reinforced by the Anglo-French Declaration of 7 November 1918,[12] which was issued by the British military commands in Palestine, Syria and Iraq, and given even wider publicity than the Declaration to the Seven. This said that the goal of the British and French governments was the complete and final liberation of peoples oppressed by the Turks, and the setting up of national governments and administrations which should derive their authority from the free exercise of the initiative and choice of the indigenous populations. Declarations of this kind by the Powers raised the expectations not only of the Arabs of Syria and Iraq, but of the Egyptians and of all peoples in the world who were living under some form of colonial or imperial rule.

It was not only fears of British and French imperial ambitions which raised doubts about the sincerity of their belief in government by consent. On 2 November 1917— shortly before the revelation of the Sykes–Picot agreement —there had been another British statement of policy involving the Near East. This was the Balfour Declaration which took the form of a letter from the British Foreign Secretary to Lord Rothschild, a leading British Jew, and read as follows :

His Majesty's Government view with favour the establishment in Palestine of a National Home for the Jewish people, and will use their best endeavours to facilitate the achievement of this object, it being clearly understood that nothing shall be done which may prejudice the civil and religious rights of existing non-Jewish communities in Palestine, or the rights and political status enjoyed by Jews in any other country.[13]

The motives behind the British government's action in supporting the adolescent Zionist movement against the opposition of the majority of British Jews and of the only Jew in the Cabinet—Edwin Montagu—were varied. On the practical side there was the hope of securing support for the Allies from Zionists in Germany and Austria (where Zionism had originated) who might otherwise have been attracted by the Central Powers' promises of support and repelled by Russian anti-semitism. British statesmen probably held the exaggerated view of the economic power and influence of world Jewry which was common at that time. They also saw an advantage of having a friendly community in Palestine, since the war had revealed the vulnerability of the Suez Canal. The Prime Minister, Lloyd George, had close friendly relations with the leading British Zionist, Chaim Weizmann (later the first President of Israel); and the Zionists, who were strongly opposed to the internationalisation of Palestine, were prepared to work for a British protectorate over the Holy Land in return for British support for Zionism. The most recent researches have shown that Sir Mark Sykes, who was delegated by Lloyd George to negotiate with the Zionists, played a key role in persuading the Cabinet to accept the idea.[14] On the idealistic side, several British ministers who, even if they were agnostic in their views, had all been brought up in the spirit of nineteenth-century bible-reading Protestantism, were attracted by the romantic idea of helping the Jewish people to return to their promised land after two thousand years.

Whatever the motives of the British government, their action was remarkable in view of the objective facts about Palestine at that time. The number of Jews in Palestine was about 60,000 out of a total population of 750,000 who were mostly Arabs. Yet the Balfour Declaration refers to the 93 per cent majority as the 'non-Jewish communities'. When the Declaration was made Palestine was still in Turkish hands; Jerusalem was to fall a month later. Even among the small Jewish community in Palestine the Zionists were a minority, as they were in the rest of the world where most Jews were either neutral or actively hostile to Zionism at that time.

Balfour and his colleagues could not foresee the future course of events. Great powers were accustomed to feeling that they could decide the developments in areas under their control. They must have had more than an inkling of the reality of Zionist objectives in Palestine. In fact they withstood the Zionist demand for a declaration in favour of the establishment of *the* national home for the Jews in Palestine rather than *a* national home—a significant difference. The Zionists accepted less than their demands for tactical reasons, but they never abandoned their objective which was the creation of a state with a Jewish majority and a Zionist character in Palestine. They pursued this aim with tenacity and dedication until they achieved it thirty years later.[15]

There is clear evidence that one key figure on the British side was fully aware that the Arabs were being deceived both with regard to the implications of the Declaration and the various pledges of self-determination for the peoples of the former Ottoman provinces. This was Balfour himself. In a memorandum he wrote on Syria, Palestine and Iraq in August 1919 he pointed out that in Syria the populations had no choice other than to accept a French-controlled administration after the war. He added :

The contradiction between the letter of the Covenant and the policy of the Allies is even more flagrant in the case of the independent nation of Palestine than in that of the independent nation of Syria. For in Palestine we do not propose even to go through the form of consulting the wishes of the present inhabitants of the country, though the American Commission * has been going through the form of seeing what they are. The four great powers are committed to Zionism and Zionism, be it right or wrong, good or bad, is rooted in age-long tradition, in present needs, in

* The King–Crane Commission. See below, p. 52.

future hopes, of far profounder import than the desires and prejudices of the 700,000 Arabs who now inhabit that ancient land.

In my opinion that is right. What I have never been able to understand is how it can be harmonised with the (Anglo-French) declaration, the Covenant, or the instructions to the Commission of Enquiry. . . .

In fact, so far as Palestine is concerned, the powers have made no statement of fact that is not admittedly wrong, and no declaration of policy which, at least in the letter, they have not always intended to violate.[16]

Article 22 of the Covenant specifically referred to 'Certain communities formerly belonging to the Turkish Empire' having reached a stage of development where 'their existence as independent nations can be provisionally recognised subject to the rendering of administrative advice and assistance by a mandatory until such time as they are able to stand alone'. The declared purpose of the mandate system created during the 1919 peace settlement was that one of the Powers should assist a former colonial territory to achieve full independence through the establishment of representative institutions. It was most definitely not intended to create new imperial possessions.

Balfour was writing during the Paris Peace Conference, and much had already happened since the conflicting pledges to Arabs and Jews had been made. The announcement of the Balfour Declaration added to King Hussein's fears raised by the earlier signs of Anglo-French intentions, and once again he asked the British government for an explanation. Commander D. G. Hogarth, the head of the Arab Bureau in General Allenby's headquarters, was despatched to Jedda. Hogarth pressed the case for the return of the Jews to Palestine, but King Hussein was already showing perceptive anxiety that the Balfour Declaration might foreshadow a Jewish state in Palestine. Hogarth reported : 'The King would not accept an independent Jewish State in Palestine, nor was I instructed to warn him that such a

state was contemplated.' The King accepted Hogarth's
assurances, such as they were, and ended by showing enthusiasm for the advantages that Jewish immigration would
bring to the Arab countries.[17]

The truth was that King Hussein had no alternative to
accepting Britain's assurances, in view of the weakness of his
position. France, with her Arab possessions in North Africa
and her determined ambitions in Syria and Lebanon, was
deeply suspicious of the Arab nationalist movement and
positively hostile towards the Hashemite family. That
Hussein needed Britain's support became immediately
apparent when only British intervention against strong
French opposition secured a place at the Paris Peace Conference for his son Feisal. It was made clear that he represented only the Hejaz and not the Arabs as a whole. Feisal,
who had met Chaim Weizmann in June 1918 and been
assured like his father that the Zionists did not aim to
establish a Jewish state in Palestine, reached an agreement
with Weizmann in London in November 1918 which they
both signed in the following January. This provided for
'all necessary measures' to encourage large scale Jewish
immigration into Palestine and the despatch of a Zionist
commission to Palestine to report upon the best measures
for developing the economic potential of 'the Arab State'.
However, Feisal was able to add a codicil which was signed
by both parties as follows : 'Provided the Arabs obtain their
independence as demanded . . . I shall concur in the above
articles. But if the slightest modification or departure were
to be made, I shall not then be bound by a single word of
the present Agreement. . . .'[18]

From a very weak position Feisal attempted to retrieve
what he could of Arab aspirations in Paris. Taking his stand
on the doctrines of self-determination preached by President
Wilson and restated in the Anglo-French Declaration, he
proposed that a commission of enquiry be sent out to Syria
and Palestine to examine the wishes of its inhabitants.

President Wilson enthusiastically accepted the proposal, and his suggestion that the commission should consist of French, British, Italian and American members was endorsed by the Conference. But in reality the French were strongly hostile to the Commission while the British were lukewarm. Eventually all the parties except the Americans withdrew. The American appointees, Henry King and Charles Crane, decided to go on their own, and their report fully explains British and French hostility towards the Commission. After exhaustive consultations with the inhabitants of Syria they reported that while the overwhelming majority opposed the mandatory system, they acknowledged the need for outside assistance, provided it came first from the United States or, as second choice, from Britain.[19] On no account did they want it from France. Realising that the mandatory system was inevitable, the Commission recommended that the United States should have the mandate for Syria, and Britain for Iraq, provided the mandate was of limited duration and that the mandatory was in no sense a colonising power. They also recommended that Feisal should become King of Syria and that Iraq should have an Arab monarch. On the Zionist question they declared themselves to have set out with a strong disposition in favour of Zionism and to have found much to approve of in the Zionists' aspirations and plans, but to have concluded that the 'extreme Zionist programme must be greatly modified if the civil and religious rights of the non-Jewish inhabitants of Palestine were to be protected in accordance with the terms of the Balfour Declaration'. After discussions with Zionist leaders in Jerusalem they had no doubt 'that the Zionists looked forward to a practically complete dispossession of the present non-Jewish inhabitants of Palestine, by various forms of purchase'.

The King–Crane Commission's report was ignored by the Allies. It was clearly repugnant to Britain and France, and the United States, after raising so many expectations, was

shortly to retreat into a long period of isolation. Meanwhile
Britain and France had been holding their own belated
discussions about the future of the Middle East.[20] A serious
rift between the two Allies still seemed possible. The British
Government regarded French ambitions in Syria as exces-
sive—a view held most strongly by the leading British
Arabists such as T. E. Lawrence—but was anxious not to
appear to be aiming merely to take France's place. It also
had a certain feeling of obligation, which was not in the
least shared by the French, towards King Hussein and the
Arabs. When Clemenceau wanted to garrison Syria with
French troops Lloyd George refused to agree.

Meanwhile the former al-Fatat society had taken the
initiative by forming an Arab Independence Party which
gained Feisal's support on his return from Paris in May
1919. Elections were held wherever possible throughout
Syria—although they were blocked by the French in
O.E.T.A. West—and a General Syrian Congress meeting in
Damascus called for recognition of the independence of
Syria (including Palestine) and Iraq, and the repudiation of
both the Sykes–Picot Agreement, the Balfour Declaration
and the mandatory system.[21] But the realities of power soon
asserted themselves. When Feisal returned to Europe in
August his weakness forced him to accept urgent British
advice that he should reach an agreement with Clemenceau. In November 1919 Feisal went to Paris and reached
a provisional agreement with the French Premier pending
the final settlement, providing for French occupation of the
Syrian coastal areas and a French monopoly of assistance
to the Arab State in the interior. Feisal was aware that many
of his followers would refuse to accept these terms but he
knew the weakness of his position and he still hoped for
British and American support for his cause in the final
settlement of the Peace Conference.

Feisal returned to Syria to try in vain to persuade his
followers that he had not accepted the dismemberment of

Syria. They were in no mood for compromise and on 8 March 1920 the General Syrian Congress passed a resolution proclaiming the independence of Syria (including Palestine and Lebanon but with internal autonomy provided for Lebanon) under Feisal as King. At the same time a similar meeting of Iraq leaders declared Iraq's independence with the Amir Abdullah as King.

Britain and France reacted swiftly. Declaring that they did not recognise the Damascus resolutions, they hastily convened a meeting of the Supreme Council of the League of Nations which made its decisions on 25 April and announced them on 5 May. Greater Syria was to be partitioned into the two French mandates of Lebanon and Syria and the British mandate of Palestine, while Iraq was to remain undivided as a British mandate. The British mandate for Palestine carried with it the obligation to carry out the terms of the Balfour Declaration.

The Arabs of Syria were thoroughly aroused by the announcement of these decisions and urged Feisal to declare war on the French. Aware of his military weakness, Feisal refused, but he allowed his more hotheaded younger officers to carry out attacks on French positions near the Lebanese border. The French commander-in-chief, General Gouraud, sent an ultimatum on 14 July demanding that French forces be allowed to occupy Aleppo, Homs, Hama and the Bekaa plain between the mountains of Lebanon and anti-Lebanon. Feisal and the General Syrian Congress accepted the ultimatum, but their action was fruitless because the French had already made up their minds. A French column including Senegalese and North African Arab troops, advanced and took Damascus on 25 July. Syrian forces, backed by the entire population of Damascus, bravely attempted resistance, but could do little against French tanks and planes. The French then invited Feisal to leave Syria. He went to Italy, and at the end of the year to London at the invitation of the British government. The British had a bad conscience about the fate of Feisal's short-lived Syrian kingdom. Winston Churchill, Secretary of State for the Colonies, told the Imperial Conference the following year that the spectacle of the French operations against Syria 'conducted very largely by black African troops' had been 'extremely painful to British opinion' but 'we have these strong ties with the French and they have to prevail, and we were not able to do anything to help the Arabs in the matter. . . .'[22]

One of the first acts of France, which on its own insistence had been awarded the mandate for Syria and Lebanon at San Remo, was to create the Grand Liban by enlarging Lebanon at Syria's expense. Lebanon included the Maronite Catholics and other Christian sects who traditionally looked on France as their protector, whereas Syria was a centre of Arab nationalism. The French purpose was to make an enlarged and strengthened Lebanon the base for its Near Eastern policy. General Gouraud's decree of 31 August 1920 added to the former autonomous Sanjak of Lebanon (that is Mount Lebanon) the coastal towns of Tripoli to the north, Sidon and Tyre to the south and the Bekaa plain to the east. The population of the Grand Liban had a small Christian majority, but with the higher Muslim birth-rate they were in constant danger of becoming a minority.

The decisions of the San Remo Conference were not carried out without considerable bloodshed. Apart from the fighting in Syria, there was an uprising against the Jews by Muslim and Christian Arabs in Palestine, alarmed by the statements of the Zionist leaders, who had already set up their organisation in Jerusalem and were making their objectives clear. The Palestinian Arabs had enjoyed considerable autonomy under the Turks and held high posts in their administration. They had not been enthusiastic supporters of the Arab Revolt, but they were now united in their fear and dislike of Zionism.[23] In Iraq also, where Arab hopes had been thwarted by the establishment of an Anglo-Indian administration with virtually no Arab participation, there was a major uprising of the tribes of the Euphrates in the summer of 1920, which cost the British over 2,000 casualties and £40 million (more than three times the total subsidies for the Arab Revolt) to suppress. Understandably, the year 1920 was referred to by the Arabs as '*Am al-Nakhba* (the year of disaster).

The need for economy prompted Britain to act, and in March 1921 Winston Churchill, Secretary of State for the Colonies, with T. E. Lawrence as his adviser, held a conference in Cairo. The conference was all-British and included the newly appointed High Commissioner for Palestine, Sir Herbert Samuel (an early Zionist sympathiser who later attracted considerable Zionist odium by trying to reconcile Arab and Jewish interests in Palestine).[24] It was decided to carry out the arrangement already prepared with the Amir Feisal in London by making him King of Iraq. A special problem had been created by the Amir Abdullah who, disappointed in his hopes for a throne in Iraq, had appeared in Maan at the head of some tribal forces in November 1920 and was allegedly contemplating an attack on the French in Syria to avenge his brother Feisal. It is doubtful whether this was his real intention, but his presence was a sufficient embarrassment to cause Churchill to confer with him in Jerusalem. Churchill rejected Abdullah's various proposals for the incorporation of Transjordan (that is the east bank of the River Jordan) either into Iraq or Palestine under an Arab administration, but a provisional arrangement was reached whereby Britain agreed to recognise Abdullah as Amir of Transjordan with an annual British subsidy until Britain could persuade France to restore an Arab state in Syria with Abdullah at its head. Since the French had no such intention the provisional arrangement became permanent, and the state of Transjordan came into existence until it was incorporated with the West Bank of Jordan following the first Arab–Israeli war (1948–49) to form the Hashemite kingdom of Jordan.

The mandates for Palestine, Syria and Lebanon were formally approved by the Council of the League of Nations in July 1922 and became effective in September 1923. In 1924 the United States gave its approval to the mandates. Article 2 of the Palestine mandate laid on the mandatory the responsibility for placing the country under such political, administrative, and economic conditions as would secure the establishment of a Jewish National Home without prejudice to the rights and position of the rest of the population.[25] Transjordan was added to the mandated territory, but the mandatory was permitted to exclude it, and in fact did exclude it, from the area of Jewish settlement. In 1922 Transjordan was constituted a semi-autonomous Arab principality under the Amir Abdullah, subject under mandate to the British High Commission in Jerusalem.

In Iraq Sir Percy Cox, the first High Commissioner, ended military rule in October 1920 (following the suppression of the rebellion) and established an Arab Council of State advised by British officials. This was little more than an Arab façade for British rule, but a step towards self-government had been made. The British carefully prepared the ground for the Amir Feisal's accession to the throne, which was approved by the Council of State and confirmed by a plebiscite. He was enthroned on 23 August 1921. Britain decided to incorporate its obligation towards the League of Nations in a treaty, which was ratified by the Iraqi Government on 10 October 1922 against the determined opposition of nationalist elements. They insisted that the treaty should terminate the mandate and British influence, whereas in fact it incorporated the provisions of the mandate, gave guarantees on judicial matters to make up for the abolition of the Capitulations, and guaranteed Britain's special interests in Iraq.[26] Its period of validity, twenty years, was reduced the following year to four years from the ratification of peace with Turkey, which followed in July 1923. But the frontiers between Turkey and Iraq remained to be decided. In December 1925 the Council of the League of Nations awarded the Vilayet of Mosul to Iraq. In July 1926 a treaty between Turkey, Britain and Iraq accepted the new frontiers as definitive and inviolable, while Iraq agreed to pay to Turkey ten per cent of oil royalties for twenty-five years.[27]

Within a few years of the end of the war the Arab provinces of the Ottoman Empire had been partitioned and their political status decided. Five new states had emerged—Syria, Lebanon, Transjordan, Iraq and Palestine—under the tutelage of Britain and France, which had also been chiefly responsible for establishing the shape of their frontiers. It was only in the Arabian peninsula itself that the Arabs were able to preserve a large measure of independence. With the treaty of Mudros (1918) Turkish suzerainty over Yemen, which had never been very effective, finally came to an end. The country's remoteness and inaccessibility ensured that it would remain backward but free. While Hussein was King of the Hejaz, most of the rest of the peninsula was controlled by Ibn Saud who soon set about extending his rule to the remaining areas that were not under British protection. In 1919 Ibn Saud's Wahhabi warriors defeated King Hussein's army; in 1920 they captured the Asir province between the Hejaz and Yemen, and in 1921 they finally defeated the last of the Rashidi amirs, his powerful rivals in Ottoman times. Britain, which was still paying a subsidy to both Hussein and Ibn Saud, tried to persuade them to compromise, but failed and in 1924 the Wahhabis invaded the Hejaz and captured Mecca. Hussein abdicated in favour of his eldest son Ali and retired, a bitter exile, to Cyprus. But Ali's situation was hopeless. Medina and Jedda surrendered, and in January 1926 Ibn Saud was proclaimed King of the Hejaz. The Soviet Union was the first country to recognise him. Britain also acknowledged his new status in the following year through the Treaty of Jedda, in which Ibn Saud recognised in return

the Hashemites, Abdullah and Feisal, as rulers of Trans-
jordan and Iraq and the British-protected status of the
Persian Gulf sheikhdoms. In 1932 he assumed the title of
King of Saudi Arabia.

There was irony, which the Arabs of the Fertile Crescent
bitterly noted, in the fact that the parts of the Arab world
which had achieved independence following the break-up of
the Ottoman Empire were the most socially, culturally and
economically backward, while the more sophisticated areas
were placed under the control of western Christian nations.
This anomaly was even more glaring in the case of Egypt,
which had even enjoyed a large measure of independence
within the Ottoman Empire for some eighty years before
the British occupation in 1882. We have seen how the fiction
of Turkish suzerainty was finally removed in 1914 when
Britain declared Egypt a Protectorate but without formally
incorporating Egypt into the Empire. Strictly speaking
Egypt was a non-belligerent in the war, but under martial
law and the occupation of a huge allied force it was neutral
only in name. Egyptian troops helped to defend the Canal
zone against the Turks, some 150,000 Egyptians served in
the Canal Transport Service and the Auxiliary Labour
Corps and suffered severe casualties. The social effects of
the war were devastating. While some of the big landowners
and a new property-owning middle class grew rich from
war profits, the mass of the population suffered severely
from inflation, food shortages and the army's commandeer-
ing of their camels and donkeys. In 1918 the death rate
actually exceeded the birth rate in Egypt.[28]

In 1917 the elderly Sultan Hussein Kamel had died and
was replaced with British approval by his cousin Fuad, a
son of the Khedive Ismail, who had presided over the opening of the Suez Canal in 1869. Fuad was unsatisfactory because he had been brought up in Italy and had little understanding or knowledge of Egypt, but there was no obvious
alternative. He would have liked to have made himself a

fully independent ruler, but unfortunately he was incapable of representing the feelings and aspirations of the Egyptians which was to prove a serious failing in the aftermath of the war. A strong Egyptian nationalist movement had developed in the last years of the nineteenth century especially during the brief career of the charismatic Mustafa Kamel (1874–1908). It was directed against the British occupation rather than the Turks. Mustafa Kamel himself held pro-Turkish and pan-Islamic views. But although Egyptian nationalism had little connection with pan-Arabism, the relatively free intellectual atmosphere in Egypt enabled Arab writers and thinkers from outside Egypt to publish their views.

Lord Cromer retired in 1907 and was succeeded by Sir Eldon Gorst whose mild liberal experiments in giving Egyptians a greater share of political power were cut short by his early death in 1911. He in turn was succeeded as British Consul-General by Lord Kitchener, who restored a Cromerian type of paternalistic régime. Martial law and the presence of allied forces effectively prevented any manifestation of Egyptian nationalism during the war, but the underlying feelings remained, and they found a new voice in Saad Zaghlul, who had received Cromer's approval as an ideally moderate type of nationalist. Initially he was prepared to co-operate with the British occupiers, but he was to become an extreme opponent of the British and spokesman for unfettered independence.

Zaghlul had held ministerial office before the war, but had resigned and spent the war years building up his popular following. Two days after the Armistice Zaghlul made a formal request to go to London with a delegation (*Wafd*, as his political party came to be known) to present Egypt's case. The British Foreign Minister, who was preoccupied with the Paris Peace Conference, curtly refused to see Zaghlul, whom he regarded as an irresponsible extremist, or even the Egyptian Prime Minister, Rushdi Pasha, and his colleagues. In a dispatch to the British High Commissioner

in Egypt he said that, although the British Government
favoured as always giving Egyptians an increasing share in
the government, 'as you are well aware, the stage has not
yet been reached at which self-government is possible'.[29]
The British government regarded Egypt as a vital link in
imperial communications with India and the Far East which
must at all costs be kept under British control. The Egyptians on the other hand considered that their co-operation
with the Allies in the war gave them at the very least the
right to put forward their case for independence. It seemed
ludicrous to them that the desert tribesmen of Arabia should
be represented at the Paris Peace Conference but not the
Egyptians with their long political experience.

Balfour later agreed that Rushdi could come to London
after all, but the Prime Minister could do nothing without
Zaghlul, the popular leader, and resigned. When Zaghlul
began to rouse public indignation the British made use of
martial law, which was still in force, to remove him by force
to Malta. This was the signal for a violent national uprising
which Egyptians know as the 1919 Revolution. It began in
Cairo with strikes by students and government officials and
spread to the countryside. It was put down only by swift and
firm action by the depleted British forces in Egypt.

A surprised and dismayed British government sent out
Allenby, the hero of the Middle East campaigns, as High
Commissioner with special powers to restore order. Despite
his authoritarian manner, Allenby held fairly liberal views
which favoured allowing the Egyptians to manage their own
affairs as far as possible. Realising the extent of Zaghlul's
popularity he ordered his release from exile. But the problem
remained of reconciling Egyptian aspirations with those
British interests which were regarded in London as vital.
The British government's solution was to send out a mission
headed by the Colonial Secretary, Lord Milner.

Few men had more faith in the British Empire than
Milner, but he soon realised that the protectorate over

o.e.s.—3*

Egypt could not be maintained, and that the best hope was
to abolish it through an Anglo-Egyptian treaty guaranteeing
British interests. These were principally the right to maintain troops in Egypt to protect the Suez Canal, the protection of foreign interests in Egypt (that is the Capitulations)
and the status of the Sudan. This last was nominally an
Anglo-Egyptian Condominium but British officials held all
the senior government posts and decided policy. Egyptian
nationalists were now demanding a reassertion of Egyptian
authority in the Sudan, but the British government, with the
full support of Anglo-Sudanese officials, had no intention of
allowing its enlightened, if paternalistic, administration of
the Sudan to be modified.

The problem was to persuade a representative Egyptian
to sign a treaty of 'limited independence' of this kind for
Egypt. If Zaghlul refused there was no one else who could
or would take the responsibility, and after some hesitation
Zaghlul did refuse. As unrest and violence continued Allenby, seeing there was no way out of the deadlock, persuaded
a reluctant and divided British cabinet to make a unilateral
declaration of Egyptian independence reserving the un-
solved questions as special points to be settled by agreement
at some future date.[30]

The key problems between Britain and Egypt had been
shelved but not solved. Egypt had been granted a form of
semi-independence which was not accepted as final by any
representative Egyptian. However, the declaration did mean
that Egypt at once acquired many of the aspects and institutions of self-government. The Sultan Fuad became King
Fuad I; a parliamentary constitution on the Belgian model
was introduced which gave the King considerable powers,
although not enough for his liking, and the number of
British officials in Egypt was steadily reduced. But the
British Army remained in occupation and British officers
retained key posts in the Egyptian army. The status of the
British High Commissioner, who retained his power to inter-

vene in many of Egypt's internal affairs as well as his title, was still very different from that of the other foreign ambassadors who now came to Cairo.

There were now three major political forces in Egypt: the King, Zaghlul's Wafd Party and the British, with the last holding ultimate authority. In the years 1922-36 the same pattern repeated itself several times. The King would dissolve parliament or suspend the constitution and rule for a time through ministers of his own choice. When popular feeling was so aroused that he could do so no longer, elections would be held in which the Wafd invariably won a sweeping victory. But although the Wafd was unquestionably the popular national party, the 1922 constitution, which gave it power, failed to provide a satisfactory and stable basis of Egypt's political life. The Wafd was a coalition of forces which included a minority with a clear idea of the kind of social and economic reforms that Egypt needed. But the party as a whole was dominated by the wealthy landowners who opposed these reforms, while the leading Wafdist politicians were so heavily engaged in the struggle for power with the King and the British that they had no time or energy to prove that the parliamentary system could satisfy Egypt's needs. Liberal constitutionalism on the European model failed to take root in Egypt.

4 Turkey Resurgent

THE Ottoman Empire had been dismembered and dissolved, but what of Turkey itself? After the Bolshevik Revolution Turkey had joined with its allies in concluding a peace treaty with the Soviet leaders at Brest-Litovsk (3 March 1918)[1] by which Turkey regained all the territories lost to Russia including those ceded in 1877. But in every other respect the year 1918 was disastrous, as one by one the Ottoman provinces fell to the Allies. Mustafa Kemal (1881–1938) headed a section of army leaders who favoured abandoning what remained of the Empire and withdrawing to Anatolia to create a nation in the Turkish homeland. His advice was rejected by Enver Pasha, and with the final defeat Kemal was left to extricate the Seventh Army from Palestine and bring it back to Anatolia with the remaining eastern armies.

The new Sultan, Mohammed VI (Mohammed V had died in July 1918), dissolved the Turkish parliament and formed a new government of men who were ready to accept the terms of the Allies who were preparing for the dismemberment of Turkey. Apart from the Allied military administration of Istanbul (as Constantinople was now more generally called), the French occupied Cilicia and Adana, British forces took over the Dardanelles and Samsun on the Black Sea and the Italians landed at Antalya. The C.U.P. had collapsed and its leaders fled. The Sultan now decided to crush the remnants of the Young Turks. Mustafa Kemal, who already enjoyed high prestige in Turkey, was causing the Sultan and his government trouble by organising resistance to the Allies in Istanbul, so Mohammed VI appointed him Inspector-General of the Ninth Army based on Samsun with orders to disband what remained of the Ottoman forces.

Mustafa Kemal landed at Samsun on 9 May 1919, but instead of disbanding the army he gathered supporters for the declaration of a Turkish state free from foreign control. On 19 May the Allies allowed a large Greek force to land at Izmir and occupy the surrounding district. The Italians also had a claim to Izmir and the Allies wished to forestall them, but Greek ambitions went much further, to the annexation of the whole of western Anatolia in which there were substantial Greek minorities 'and thus bring nearer the "Great Idea"—the restoration of the departed glories of the Greek Christian Empire of Constantinople'.[2]

While the Sultan ordered the Turkish troops not to resist the Greeks, Kemal was rapidly gathering support for the cause of Turkish independence. A conference called at Erzurum of all organisations supporting the idea elected him chairman, and on 23 April he became president of a new national assembly, meeting at Ankara which had become the centre of national resistance. Although exhausted by eight years of almost continuous warfare the Turkish people were roused to pursue the struggle by the Greek advance into the Anatolian heartland. They rejected the harsh terms of the Treaty of Sèvres of August 1920,[3] which would have left Turkey helpless and deprived of some of its richest provinces, and the Sultan, now little more than an Allied puppet, was increasingly discredited.

The Greco-Turkish war lasted two years : 1920–2. At first the Turks, exhausted and ill-equipped, were unable to halt the Greek advance, but in 1921 the tide turned with a great Turkish victory on the River Sakarya. In 1922 the Greeks, weakened by dissension at home, were in headlong retreat, and in September Mustafa Kemal reoccupied Izmir. When Mustafa Kemal's forces crossed the Dardanelles to drive the Greeks out of European Turkey also, a direct clash with

Britain was only narrowly averted. The Allies gave way to a resurgent Turkey and by the terms of the armistice, to which Greece also adhered, they recognised Turkish sovereignty over Istanbul, the Straits and eastern Thrace.

The peace conference which followed culminated with the Treaty of Lausanne of 24 July 1923 [4] recognising full Turkish sovereignty in nearly all the territories which are now those of the Turkish Republic. At the same time the hated Capitulations were finally abolished. Thus the Treaty of Sèvres, which had been much more severe in its terms for Turkey than those offered to Germany at Versailles, was set aside and Turkey finally emerged from the war and its aftermath in a better position than any of its defeated allies. Although a considerable body of Turkish opinion favoured the retention of a constitutional monarchy, Mustafa Kemal was determined to get rid of the Sultan, and his prestige and authority were such that he had his way. On 1 November 1922 the National Assembly passed a law abolishing the Sultanate and Mohammed VI fled into exile. The Assembly took over full powers. On 29 October 1923 Turkey was proclaimed a Republic with Kemal as President. He also founded the Republican Party to unite the various groups who had supported his struggle for Turkish independence.

The Islamic caliphate attracted as much loyalty as the sultanate and, although Mustafa Kemal would have liked to abolish the two offices together, he bowed to the popular will in this matter. He agreed that Mohammed VI's nephew, Abdul-Megid, should become the spiritual head of Islam. But, although the Caliph was shorn of all political power his court became the centre of monarchist intrigue, and when two prominent Indian Muslims, Amir Ali and the Aga Khan, published a statement calling upon the Turkish people to preserve the caliphate, Mustafa Kemal made use of the unfavourable reaction among Turkish nationalist opinion against this foreign interference to abolish it. A bill to this effect was passed by the Assembly on 3 March 1924.[5]

The title of Caliph has not since been revived. The assumption by King Hussein of the Hejaz of the title was not recognised except in the Hejaz, Transjordan, and Iraq and lapsed some months later with his abdication. In May 1926 a caliphate congress held in Cairo was attended by delegates from thirteen Muslim countries (not including Turkey) but was inconclusive. Since then the caliphate has not been an issue in Islamic politics.

Mustafa Kemal was an ardent secular nationalist without religious faith. He believed that all the inheritance of the Ottoman Empire should be destroyed and Turkey thoroughly modernised. This required the emancipation of women and the elimination of the social and political power of the Islamic religious authorities. Following the abolition of the caliphate the institutions of religious learning and religious courts were closed. In the following year a new legal code, which was an adapted translation of the Swiss civil, the Italian penal, and the German commercial codes, was substituted for the Islamic *Sharia*. From then on only civil marriage and divorce were recognised and polygamy became illegal. A further step was taken in 1928, when the state became officially secular, with the deletion of the clause in the constitution reading that 'the religion of the Turkish state is Islam' and establishing 'laicism' as one of the six cardinal principles of the state. An essential element of secularisation was the introduction of a Latin-based alphabet and a ban on the public use of Arabic letters. In 1933 Turkish was even substituted for the Arabic call to prayer, and Sunday replaced Friday as the weekly holiday. The fez, which Kemal regarded as a symbol of the unenlightened traditionalism which had kept Turkey backward, was abolished and replaced by western-style hats and caps. Finally in 1935 surnames on the European model were introduced. Mustafa Kemal took the name of Atatürk or *Father of the Turks*.

These secular reforms, which were backed by Atatürk's

immense authority among all sections of the Turkish people, were profound and far-reaching. But they did not mean that the Turks had renounced Islam. If the authority of the *ulema* was destroyed, the Turkish masses, who are mostly peasant farmers, preserved their Islamic faith, while even the intelligentsia of the cities would have ridiculed the idea that they had ceased to be Muslims. In their view there has only been a Turkish reformation of Islam.[6]

In some important respects the Atatürk Revolution succeeded in transforming the social and economic attitudes of the Turkish people. In others there has been little change. Finance and commerce were traditionally beneath the dignity of the Ottoman Turks, who left them to Europeans or non-Turkish Ottoman citizens, but since the Revolution Turks have been increasingly attracted to business, and today the country's trade is almost entirely in Turkish hands. Industrialisation, encouraged in the 1930s and 1940s by a system of state capitalism which was often inefficient but achieved results, has forged ahead. The share of agriculture in the Gross National Product has declined from about 70 per cent to about 30 per cent. However, agriculture still employs some 54 per cent of the population over 15, and in 1965 more than 65 per cent of the population was still officially classed as dwelling in villages. A large section of the lower urban stratum consists of villagers who have either migrated temporarily to the towns or who retain close ties with rural areas. In many of the villages of Anatolia the traditional patterns of behaviour have hardly changed.

Atatürk regarded the emancipation of women as one of his most essential reforms. After the abolition of polygamy and Islamic divorce (which is outstandingly easy for the male) women were given the right to vote and be candidates in elections. Today there is no career which is not open to the Turkish girl if her family is willing. However, the idea of equality of the sexes has not yet found general acceptance, especially in small towns and villages. ('Turkey remains largely a masculine society which looks askance at un-accompanied and unattached women. . . . In Anatolia the absence of women from coffee houses and eating places is almost total. The equally marked absence of waitresses and manageresses contributes to a barrack-room atmosphere of rough-and-ready untidiness which has struck so many per-ceptive travellers.'[7])

After the closing of the religious schools, which provided most of the education which was available for Turkish Muslims, recourse was had to European models and an entirely new secular system was created. The number of children attending primary school rose from 55 per cent of those eligible in 1955 to 83 per cent in 1966. The introduc-tion of the Latin script facilitated the spread of literacy and the proportion of illiterates fell from about 80 per cent in 1935 to about 48 per cent in 1966. (About two-thirds of the illiterates are female.)

These figures tend to disguise the nature of Turkey's greatest social problem—the vast and growing gap between the standards of the towns and the countryside. The educa-tional level of the average villager is so low that the young urban teacher finds the countryside an unattractive place in which to live and work.

5 The Arab Struggle for Independence 1920–1939

ALTHOUGH Atatürk's personality and his modernising reforms attracted widespread interest in the Arab world, especially among university students and the professional classes, the dissolution of the Ottoman Empire meant that the Turkish and Arab peoples were now on separate courses. The mutual antipathy between Turks and Arabs, derived from the former imperial-colonial relationship, did not encourage intercourse between the two races, but the principal reason was that Atatürk's policies were aimed to persuade the Turkish people to forget the past glories of the Ottoman Empire and to concentrate on developing a strong modern state on European lines. Turkey showed little interest in the fate of its former Arab provinces.

Arab nationalism, on the other hand, was no longer concerned with asserting itself against the Turks but against western Christian domination. Many Arabs suffered a rude awakening. The Ottoman Empire had helped to protect much of the Arab world against non-Muslim encroachments for nearly four centuries, and, despite the later attempts to centralise the administration in Constantinople, the Arab provinces had enjoyed a large measure of autonomy. One view of the dangers to Islam of the dissolution of the Ottoman Empire was expressed by the Aga Khan, who headed a deputation of prominent Muslims to the British Prime Minister, Lloyd George, during the Peace Conference. Years later he wrote in his *Memoirs* :

The reasons for Muslim concern were profound and historic —Turkey stood almost alone in the world of that time as the sole surviving independent Muslim nation; with all its shortcomings, the imperial régime in Constantinople was a visible and enduring reminder of the temporal greatness of Islam's achievements. In the Caliphate there was, too, for all of the Sunni sect or persuasion, a spiritual link of the utmost significance. . . .

Muslim opposition to the break-up of the Turkish Empire had a basis—however much misunderstood it may have been—of true statesmanship and of understanding of the absorbing political realities of the Middle East. First, we felt that the separation of the Arabs from the Turks (hailed at the time as emancipation from a tyranny, although within a few years all Arab nationalists were singing a very different tune) would not lead to the emergence of a single strong Arab nation extending from Egypt to Persia and from Alexandretta to Aden and the Indian Ocean. We foresaw in large measure what actually happened : the formation of a number of small Arab nations, for many years of little more than colonial status, under British and French overlordship. We predicted that the Arabs would in fact merely be changing masters, and where these masters had been Muslim Turks they would now be Christians, or (as ultimately happened in a large part of Palestine) Jews. . . .[1]

The Aga Khan's doubts were fully realised. So far from the liberation of the Arabs from Ottoman domination leading to a revival of their former power and greatness, their energies for at least the next forty years were devoted to asserting their independence from the west. In the first stage it was largely a question of claiming their right to manage their internal affairs, but, even when this had been broadly achieved by the 1950s, the weak and divided Arab states were still regarded as part of the western satellite system and had to fight to pursue an independent foreign policy. Finally, the tragic consequences of the establishment of a Zionist state in Palestine, with western support and against the wishes of the indigenous Arab majority, ensured that the Arabs' struggle with the west was not resolved, but continued to absorb a large part of their creative powers.

The Arabs were soon made forcefully aware of what had been lost by the destruction of the Ottoman Empire. Any hopes of the establishment of a unified Arab state under Hashemite rule were already shattered by 1920. The structure and boundaries of the new states that were created from the ruins of the Empire—Iraq, Syria, Lebanon, Transjordan and Palestine—were decided by the Powers with little regard for Arab wishes. These states began their existence without any sense of national cohesion or loyalty. This was to make them virtually ungovernable when they became fully independent. The mandatory powers permitted the establishment of representative institutions within narrowly prescribed limits, but these were quite incapable of reconciling the various conflicting interests within the country or of adapting themselves to rapid social change. In other words they failed in the task of building up a national political community. Since these new Arab states were western creations their people tended to regard their frontiers as artificial. Inevitably, however, a body of self-interest grew up around the independent governments in Baghdad, Beirut, Damascus and Amman. The emotional aspiration for Arab unity remained undiminished, but the obstacles to its practical achievement steadily increased.

The situation in Egypt and French North Africa, which were not strictly speaking successor states to the Ottoman Empire since they had already been outside Ottoman control for some time, was somewhat different. They had not been partners in the Arab Revolt against the Turks and had not been inspired by an ideal of a revived Arab nation. Egypt after the First World War and the Maghrib states after the Second World War were absorbed in their own struggle for independence from their British and French occupiers. Pan-Arabism as a political programme meant little to them at that stage. Moreover, the Maghrib states were divided from the eastern Arab world by the desert wastes of Libya, which has been aptly described as a 'geographical hyphen'. Nevertheless, the Arab states were all linked by a kind of common nervous system which exists because of their shared language, culture, religion and historical experience. Anything that occurs in one Arab state has repercussions elsewhere in the Arab world. Since the 1930s no Arab has remained entirely unaffected by the struggle in Palestine. In the 1950s they were all moved to some degree by the Algerian Revolution.

SYRIA AND LEBANON

The basis of French policy in its two mandated territories in the Middle East was to strengthen and promote the traditionally Francophile Christian population at the expense of the Muslim Arab elements.* But in both countries in the early years of the mandate France behaved in the manner of a colonial government backed by superior military power. The press was controlled and nationalist demonstration suppressed. The terms of the mandate promised a constitution for both countries within three years, but the Lebanese constitution, which was drafted in Paris with little consultation with the Lebanese, was imposed in 1926. It provided for a bicameral parliament and a president.[2] The principle was established that seats in parliament and the cabinet should be distributed on a basis of religious confession. The President was a Maronite Catholic and the Prime Minister a Sunni Muslim.

With the unmistakable purpose of dividing Syria in order to rule it more easily, France partitioned the country into four separate administrations based on the religious and racial minorities in each area. The great majority of Syrians, and especially the educated élite, refused to accept this

* For a fuller discussion of French policy in Syria and Lebanon see Ann Williams, *Britain and France in the Middle East and North Africa*, pp. 29–36.

partition. Many of them went further, demanding an independent Syria which should also include Palestine and
Transjordan. A serious crisis arose in 1925 when the Druzes
(an occult and distinctive sect of Islam) rose in revolt because of local grievances and formed an alliance with the
nationalists in Damascus. The revolt subsided gradually,
leaving much bitterness, but it led the French to pursue a
more conciliatory policy.

In 1930 the French High Commissioner promulgated a
new constitution which made Syria, like Lebanon, a parliamentary republic, but with France retaining control over
foreign affairs and security.[3]

The new constitutions failed to satisfy nationalist opinion
even in Lebanon. The Lebanon constitution was suspended
from 1932 to 1937 and the Syrian constitution from 1933
to 1936. Various factors contributed to a new French effort
at conciliation in 1936. An Anglo-Iraqi treaty had brought
Iraq to independence in 1932, and an Anglo-Egyptian
Treaty was finally concluded in 1936. The expanding power
of Fascist Italy and the outbreak of the Spanish Civil War
had raised tension throughout the Mediterranean, and in
France a left-wing Popular Front Government had come to
power. A treaty was signed in September 1936 providing
for Syrian independence, Franco-Syrian consultation on
foreign policy, French priority in advice and assistance, and
the retention by France of two military bases. The Jebal
Druze and Latakia districts were to be incorporated into
Syria.

A similar treaty was negotiated with Lebanon in November, but, although both treaties were ratified by the Syrian
and Lebanese parliaments, they were never ratified by the
French Chamber and remained inoperative.[4] The Popular
Front Government fell from power and was replaced by
more conservative interests, which favoured retaining
French control over the Levant states for strategic and
economic reasons. There were prospects of the discovery of

oil in north-eastern Syria, and the two countries were a convenient stepping-stone on the route to the Far East. Another important factor was that Syrian and Lebanese independence would profoundly influence the Arabs in French Africa. With the growing threat from Nazi Germany with its population of 80 millions compared with France's 40 millions, France felt the need more than ever to draw on the manpower of its North African possessions.

The prospect of war with Germany also led France to conciliate Turkey over the question of Alexandretta, which was claimed by the Turks. In 1937 the Sanjak was given an autonomous status, and after a Franco-Turkish commission had ensured a Turkish majority in parliamentary elections, although Arabs and Armenians outnumbered Turks in the population, France agreed to the absorption of the Sanjak of Alexandretta by Turkey (which was renamed the Hatay) in June 1939.[5]

The achievements of the French mandatory in Syria and Lebanon were far from negligible. It introduced a relatively modern administrative system, customs organisation, land registration and cadastral survey. It built many roads and created a department of antiquities. Its economic efforts were limited by the chronic weakness of the French franc on which the Syrian and Lebanese currencies were based. It gave some encouragement to both agriculture and industry, but it aroused considerable resentment by its policy of granting monopolies to French companies whose profits were repatriated to France. In the educational field its achievements were more controversial. It protected the foreign mission schools and promoted French language and culture. Arab children were taught a French interpretation of history and even learned to sing 'La Marseillaise'. But in Syria at least a system of state schools was created and a University of Damascus was also established, with its teaching mainly in Arabic.

It remains true that in both countries France was continuously hampered by the need to combat the spirit of national independence with force and the suppression of public liberties. Even in Lebanon the traditionally Franco-phile elements were roused, and in 1936 the Maronite Patriarch addressed a strongly worded memorandum to the French Government criticising many aspects of the French administration. Finally the cession of the Hatay to Turkey, which the Syrians never accepted, left a lasting bitterness.

The prospect of war with Germany also led France to reconcile Turkey over the question of Alexandretta which was claimed by the Turks. In 1937 the Sanjak received autonomous status, and after a Franco-Turkish commission

IRAQ

Following the uprising of 1920 the British mandatory authorities, partly through necessity and partly through natural inclination, pursued more liberal policies. A nucleus of parliamentary institutions was created in 1924 with de-partments of state presided over by Iraqi ministers, and the powers of British officials were gradually reduced. In 1925 Iraqi Ministers became responsible to an Iraqi parlia-ment and British officials nominally became the servants of the Iraqi government. Britain was by now prepared to end the mandate provided British interests could be maintained, but a treaty was delayed by nationalist opposition to con-tinued British tutelage in a concealed form, and by disagree-ment among other League of Nations members. Finally an Anglo-Iraqi treaty was concluded in 1930 and ratified at the end of the year.[6] It provided for an Anglo-Iraqi alliance for twenty-five years during which the two countries under-took to consult each other in order to harmonise their common interests in matters of foreign policy. Britain would have the use of certain Air Force bases in Iraq and existing means of communications. In return Britain would provide a military mission to help train the Iraqi army. In accord-ance with the treaty Iraq became a member of the League of Nations in 1932, although Britain's insistence was needed to overcome the doubts of some League members about

Iraq's ability to shoulder all the burdens of independence.

By 1932 Iraq had made some progress towards the creation of a unified modern state. King Feisal I, although having gained his throne through British sponsorship, had established himself as an independent and fairly enlightened national leader. But the problems of Iraq's inherent divisiveness remained acute. About one quarter of the population were non-Arab—Kurdish, Turcoman or Assyrian—while the Arab population was divided between a Shia majority and the politically dominant Sunni minority. Tribal factionalism among the bedouin population of the deserts was also a severe challenge to the authority of the state.

King Feisal I died suddenly in 1933 and was succeeded by his son Ghazi. Handsome and popular, Ghazi was widely regarded as an Arab nationalist, but he lacked *gravitas* and authority. Rival political factions encouraged tribalism while a series of incompetent, reactionary and increasingly authoritarian cabinets succeeded each other in office. They were opposed by an alliance of reformist middle-class intellectuals and young nationalist army officers inspired by the example of Ataturk. In 1936 these seized power under the leadership of General Bakr Sidki. The movement ended ten months later, as it had begun, with assassination and a military coup.[7] It was a failure because the reformist elements were soon set aside; the army was divided and the mass of the population alienated. But it was an event of great significance because it established a precedent for military coups in the Arab world. Despite the coup's failure, the Iraqi army had gained a new self-assurance and a taste for interference in political life. The army faction which overthrew Bakr Sidki remained a power behind the scenes, capable of making or unmaking cabinets. However, in 1938 this group, known as the Seven, was instrumental in bringing to power a pro-British civilian politician, Nuri Said, who was to dominate the Iraqi state for the next twenty years through his strong personality and political finesse.

King Ghazi's death in an automobile accident on 4 April
1939 was followed by disturbances as the rumour spread
that he had been killed by the British for his nationalist
views. Nuri Said and the Seven agreed on the choice of the
Amir Abdul Ilah, nephew of Feisal I and brother of King
Ghazi's widow, as regent for the infant Crown Prince Feisal.

Iraq's economic prospects were greatly enhanced by the
discovery of a major oil field near Kirkuk in the north in
1927. From 1934 onwards oil revenues began to contribute
to the development of industry, irrigation, communications
and public services. The Iraqi oil industry was a monopoly
of the Iraq Petroleum Company (I.P.C.) and its subsidiaries
the Basrah Petroleum Company (B.P.C.) and the Mosul
Petroleum Company (M.P.C.). I.P.C. was owned jointly by
the Anglo-Iranian Oil Company (later British Petroleum),
the Royal Dutch–Shell group, an American group which
was ultimately reduced to Standard Oil of New Jersey and
Socony-Vacuum (later Mobil-Oil), and the Compagnie
Française des Pétroles (C.F.P.), with the Armenian financier
Gulbenkian owning the remaining five per cent. France's
share was a reward for relinquishing its claims to Mosul
under the Sykes–Picot agreement. American interests
secured their entrée into the Iraqi oil industry in 1928 with
strong support from the U.S. State Department, which based
its case on the British government's declared intention to
allow Iraq complete freedom of action in regard to its oil
resources.[8]

Iraqi ministers attempted to defend Iraq's interests, but
their inexperience and Iraq's subordinate political status
made it impossible for them to negotiate with the western
powers on terms of equality. The steady increase in Iraq's
oil revenues did not prevent Iraqi nationalists from resent-
ing the overbearing monopolistic powers of I.P.C. over
their country's major natural resource.

EGYPT AND SUDAN

Britain had been led to declare Egypt's independence with
several important qualifications because it had seen no
alternative, but the consequence was to leave Anglo-
Egyptian relations in a highly unsatisfactory, if not un-
manageable, situation. British dominance was reduced, but
was still sufficient to arouse the angry resentment of Egyptian nationalists under the fiery leadership of Saad Zaghlul.
Strikes, bombings and the assassination of European officials
were frequent during 1922–4. Much of the trouble centred
on the question of the Sudan, as the King and all Egyptian
political elements reasserted Egypt's claims, which Britain
strongly resisted. The Sudanese were not immune to the
Egyptian nationalist fever, which helped to foment a Sudanese uprising against British rule in 1924. But the rising
generation of Sudanese nationalists had no desire for a
resumption of Egyptian rule; this was a reality that it took
Egyptian politicians many years to accept.

The Anglo-Egyptian relations reached their first major
crisis in November 1924 with the murder in Cairo of Sir
Lee Stack, the Governor General of the Sudan, who by
convention was also Sirdar (Commander-in-Chief) of the
Egyptian army. The prompt punitive action of Allenby,
who held Zaghlul responsible, virtually eliminated Egypt's
minor share in the Condominium administration and em-
phasised the extent of Britain's residual powers in Egypt.
However, when Allenby retired in 1925 he could still be
regarded as a liberal who believed in Egyptian self-government. If he failed to reach agreement with Egyptian
nationalism it was because this would have required concessions which no British government would have allowed.
He was succeeded from 1925 to 1929 by the more imperial-
minded Lord Lloyd who fought, on the whole successfully,
to retain what was left of British control through the reten-

tion of British officials in key ministries such as finance, war and justice.

Zaghlul died in 1927 and was succeeded at the head of the Wafd by Nahas Pasha. He was a lesser man, but the Wafd remained the national party with mass popular support. In 1931 King Fuad succeeded in his aim of ousting the Wafd from power. Suspending the constitution, he called upon Sidky Pasha, an able right-wing authoritarian, who amended the electoral law to ensure the defeat of the Wafd in the elections. After two years Sidky fell ill and was succeeded by men of lesser ability; popular demand for the restoration of the 1923 constitution increased until the King was forced to agree shortly before his death. He was succeeded by his sixteen-year-old son Farouk, who was initially received with wild enthusiasm by the Egyptian masses.

On several occasions between 1924 and 1936 renewed attempts had been made to agree on an Anglo-Egyptian treaty, but they had all broken down on the question of the reserved points in the 1922 declaration of independence— especially the Sudan. But in 1936 the situation had changed. On the one hand the Wafd Party, chastened by another five years in opposition, had softened its attitude towards Britain. It had come to accept that it could not remain in office against the opposition of both the British and the palace. Britain, on the other hand, saw the advantages of dealing with politicians who had mass popular support. Both Egypt and Britain were alarmed by Mussolini's African ambitions; Anglo-Egyptian co-operation for the defence of Egypt seemed essential.

The result was the Anglo-Egyptian Treaty of 1936 which took Egypt much of the way towards full independence.[9] The Treaty was to last twenty years; both parties were committed to a further alliance in 1956, but Egypt would then have the right to submit to third-party judgement the question of whether British troops were any longer necessary in Egypt. The British occupation of Egypt was formally ended, but this did not mean that British troops would leave the country. As Egypt's self-defence capability improved they would be withdrawn gradually to the Canal zone and Sinai, where their number would be limited to 10,000 land forces and 400 air pilots. Britain reserved the right of re-occupation with unrestricted use of Egyptian ports, airports and roads in the event of war.

On the other hand Egypt gained full control over its own security forces for the first time since 1882. The British inspector-general of the Egyptian army was replaced by an Egyptian, and military intelligence was Egyptianised. It was agreed that the number of Europeans in the police should be steadily reduced. Britain sponsored Egypt's admission to the League of Nations and the British High Commissioner became an Ambassador.

It was a measure of the Wafd's anxiety for a settlement that it agreed to the shelving of the Sudanese question; the 1898 Condominium arrangement was left intact. Both sides welcomed the Treaty as a satisfactory and permanent basis for Anglo-Egyptian relations. But there was strong opposition from several quarters—especially among the students. Secure in the knowledge that it remained the only mass political party, the Wafd was scarcely aware that extra-parliamentary groups were rapidly gaining support. The most formidable of these was the Muslim Brotherhood, which had been founded by an Egyptian schoolteacher, Hussan al-Banna, as a religious revival movement, but which had become increasingly political in outlook and aims. It demanded that Egypt's entire legal, political and administrative system should be based on the Koran and Islamic tradition. The Brotherhood had established a net-work of branches which undertook the indoctrination and education of its new members. It also started para-military training for its youth groups and in the 1940s turned increasingly to terrorism. Other fascist-type groups appeared on the scene, and in response the Wafd formed its own militant organisation.

By the end of the 1930s it was apparent that Egypt's European type of parliamentary system was failing to take root. The most effective government of the inter-war years, that of Sidky Pasha, was élitist and unconstitutional while the majority party, the Wafd, was kept out of office for most of these two decades. Above all the Egyptian parliament had shown itself incapable of undertaking the kind of reforms of Egypt's social and economic structure that were urgently needed.

ARABIA AND THE PERSIAN GULF

The Arabian peninsula had been united by the political and military genius of Ibn Saud and the religious zeal of his Wahhabi followers, but his kingdom was backward and desperately poor. In the early 1920s his annual revenue from all internal sources was £150,000 with an additional British subsidy of £60,000.[10] Wahhabi puritanism frowned on all aspects of twentieth-century technological progress from the telephone to the automobile. Ibn Saud preserved the bedouin Arab tradition of retaining executive authority in his own hands, although advancing age meant that eventually he had to relax his personal control. The lack of trained Saudi Arabians caused him to recruit some of his top officials from foreign Arabs—mainly Egyptians, Syrians and Lebanese.

The King had two ways to increase his meagre revenues : to increase the fees for Muslim pilgrims to Mecca, or open the door to western exploitation. The British were opposed to the former, and he and his followers had grave doubts about the latter. In even more desperate need of funds because the world depression caused a decline in pilgrimage receipts, the King overcame his fears and granted an oil concession to Standard Oil of California. In 1933 Iraq Petroleum Company competed for the concession, but, since it already had more oil in Iraq than it knew what to do with, it was more interested in keeping potential oil lands out of the hands of a competitor than in developing them and its offer was much less substantial. Texas Oil Company, Standard Oil of New Jersey, and Socony Vacuum eventually joined with Standard Oil of California to form the Arabian American Oil Company (Aramco) in 1944.[11] A major oil field was discovered, and, although its development was held up by the war, it had already become apparent that one of the poorest Arab states was destined to become one of the richest. It was also an event of the greatest significance because the United States for the first time acquired a major interest in the Middle East.

A parallel development took place in the tiny neighbouring desert sheikhdom of Kuwait at the head of the Persian Gulf. Kuwait was under British protection, and, as in Iraq, the United States government intervened to overcome British objections to the Ruler of Kuwait granting a concession to a non-British concern. In 1934 a seventy-five-year exclusive concession was granted to the Kuwait Oil Company (K.O.C.) owned jointly by the Anglo-Iranian Oil Company and the American Gulf Oil Corporation. Oil was discovered in 1938 but, as in Saudi Arabia, development was delayed until after the Second World War.[12] Standard Oil of California and Texaco also secured an oil concession for Bahrain, where oil was discovered in 1932 and began to be exported in 1934. Although the island's oil production and revenues remained on a much more modest scale than those of Saudi Arabia and Kuwait after the Second World War, Bahrain was able to devote funds to education and social services from the 1930s and secured a lead in a generally backward area.

Rivalry between Ibn Saud and the Imam of Yemen over possession of the Asir province, which lies between Yemen and the Hejaz, led to a brief Saudi–Yemeni war in 1934. The Yemeni forces were quickly routed and a treaty of peace signed on 20 May 1934. Ibn Saud imposed only a minor frontier adjustment, and the moderation of the terms made the Imam Yahya his friend for life.[13]

In the same year Yemen signed a treaty of peace and friendship for forty years with the British government.[14] Yemen's southern frontier was accepted as the existing status quo until future negotiations could reach a final settlement. From the 1880s onwards Britain had extended its control over South Arabia through a system of treaties with the local ruling sheikhs and sultans. In 1938 the Aden Protectorate, divided administratively into the Western Protectorate and the Eastern Protectorate (the Hadhramaut) was formally established under the British Colonial Office. This provided an effective 'cordon sanitaire' protecting Aden Colony and its major port. In theory the ruling sheikhs were only bound to accept British advice, but over the years advice increasingly resembled direct administration.

Aden Colony, formerly administered by the Bombay government, was transferred to the government of India from 1932 to 1937 and then, when Indian self-government became a real prospect, to the British Colonial Office.

In spite of the Anglo-Yemeni Treaty of 1934, the Imam Yahya had not in reality abandoned his claim to suzerainty over the whole of South Arabia. His military weakness prevented a major confrontation with Britain but he continued to probe the British position in the Protectorate wherever possible. The southern frontier of Yemen was never fully established by negotiation. Many of the frontiers between the small tribal states along the eastern fringes of Arabia remained undefined. This was a matter of little consequence until the desolate peninsula was discovered to contain a large proportion of the world's oil resources and ownership of the subsoil became a question of major importance.

PERSIA (IRAN)

Persia, the Ottoman Empire's former great rival, was not a belligerent in the First World War and was not dismembered by the Allies. But, after the Anglo-Russian Agreement of 1907 had partitioned the country into British and Russian spheres of influence, Persia had continued to be the scene of fierce rivalry between the Powers with the Russians gaining the ascendancy. During the war it became a battleground for Turkish, Russian and British forces, and emerged in 1918 in a state of chaos and with an empty treasury. In 1919 the government signed with Britain an abortive agreement providing for the supply of British advisers for the administration, some military officers and equipment for a single armed force, a loan, and co-operation for the development of transport.[15]

Following the Bolshevik Revolution Russian pressure began to relax, and in February 1921 the Soviet–Persian Treaty was signed by which the Soviet government renounced 'the tyrannical policy' of tsarist Russia, remitted all Persian debts to the tsarist government, and abandoned extra-territorial privileges for Russian nationals.[16]

In 1921 Riza Shah, a colonel in the Cossack Brigade, led troops into Tehran to overthrow the government, and made himself first Minister of War and Commander-in-Chief, and then Prime Minister. In 1925 the Majlis (Parliament) voted to depose the Qajar Shah Ahmed, and Riza Shah, adopting the name Pahlevi for his family, ascended the throne in his place. In other respects Riza Shah's methods and aims bore obvious similarities to those of Atatürk. He established a strong central government, pacified the nomadic tribes, abolished the Capitulations, improved communications to unify the country (notably by building the Trans-Iranian Railway) and carried out legal reforms. He reorganised education on western lines, and in 1936 abol-

ished the veil for women and made European dress compulsory for both sexes. He also encouraged industrialisation.

Some of his economic enterprises were ill-conceived and
imposed heavy burdens of taxation on the people. His
régime became increasingly authoritarian and unpopular;
the acquisition by the crown of vast areas of land was especially resented. But there could be no doubt about Riza
Shah's achievement in uniting the country and restoring
national pride after a long period in which Persia had been
at the mercy of Great Power rivalries.

The change of mood was reflected most strikingly in the
oil industry in which Persia was the forerunner among
Middle Eastern states. Oil had been discovered in 1908 and
commercial production by the Anglo-Persian Oil Company
(later Anglo-Iranian) began in 1912. On the eve of the First
World War the British goverment, having converted the
British navy from the use of coal to oil, bought a control-
ling interest in the Company. Production rose from 1·1
million tons in 1919 to over 10 million in 1938. However,
the post-war economic depression reduced oil prices and
Persian oil revenues, and in 1923 Riza Shah denounced
the concession. The matter was referred to the League of
Nations, and was settled by an agreement in 1933 which
increased Persian royalties and reduced the concession area
from 500,000 square miles to 100,000 square miles in south-
west Persia, but in return extended the concession to 1993.
The A.I.O.C. remained a uniquely powerful economic force
in the country and a focus of nationalist resentment.[17]

PALESTINE AND TRANSJORDAN

The Palestinian mandate, which Britain had secured for
itself in the 1919 peace settlement, was to prove an impossible undertaking. The failure to solve its problems was to
poison the Arabs' relations with Britain for a generation.

(See Ann Williams, *Britain and France in the Middle East and North Africa*, pp. 24–9.)

The Balfour Declaration was incorporated within the terms of the mandate. Article 6 stated : 'The Administration of Palestine, while ensuring that the rights and position of other sections of the population are not prejudiced, shall facilitate Jewish immigration under suitable conditions and shall encourage co-operation with the Jewish agency referred to in Article 4, close settlement by Jews on the land, including State lands and waste lands not required for public purposes.'

The Zionist Organisation has established itself in Jerusalem in 1918. This later became the Jewish agency referred to in Article 4 of the mandate, which was recognised 'as a public body for the purpose of advising and co-operating with the Administration of Palestine in such economic, social and other matters as may affect the establishment of the Jewish national home....' In contrast to the Arabs, the Zionists were united, purposeful and determined. The Jewish Agency became a government within a government.

Fundamentally the Palestinian Arabs accepted neither the mandate nor the Balfour Declaration. Consequently they rejected the British High Commisioner's proposals for a limited form of representative self-government in 1923. The Zionists were equally opposed to government by elected bodies as long as they were a small minority of the population. The consequence was that self-governing institutions were never evolved for the people of Palestine for the whole period of the mandate 1922–48, although they were among the most literate and socially advanced of the inhabitants of any mandated territory.

Throughout the inter-war period the British government and its representatives in Palestine made repeated attempts to find a solution. Numerous commissions of enquiry came out from Britain and contradicted each other in the policies they advocated.

After the severe anti-Zionist rioting of the immediate post-war years Palestine was relatively peaceful from 1923 to 1929. This was because Zionist immigration had fallen away—in 1927 there was actually a net Jewish emigration out of Palestine—and Arab fears were quietened. Nevertheless the Zionists were quickly consolidating their political and economic position in the country. In August 1929 negotiations were concluded for the formation of an enlarged Jewish Agency to include non-Zionist Jewish sympathisers throughout the world. Following a renewed outbreak of violence in 1929, which arose from a dispute over religious practices at the Wailing Wall in Jerusalem, the British government acknowledged the reality of Arab fears of Zionist domination in a policy statement which seemed to favour the Arabs. At the same time a technical report stated that there was no margin of land available for new immigrants.[18] However, when this policy was reversed in an explanatory letter from the British Prime Minister, Ramsay MacDonald, to Chaim Weizmann, the president of the Jewish Agency, the Palestinian Arabs became convinced that recommendations in their favour on the spot would always be annulled in London by Zionist influence at the centre of power.

Arabs and Muslims outside Palestine were becoming increasingly aroused by the problem. In December 1931 a Muslim congress attended by delegates from twenty-two Muslim countries was called at Jerusalem to warn against the dangers of Zionism, and in 1933 a boycott of Zionist and British goods was proclaimed.

By 1931 the Jewish population had increased from 60,000 in 1919, to 175,000 or 17·7 per cent.[19] Although the Palestinian Arabs were alarmed at this increase, if the proportion of Jews had remained at this level it is conceivable that the Arabs might have come to accept a permanent Zionist minority in their midst. But, because of Hitler's accession to power in Germany, this was not to be. Between 1932 and 1938, 217,000 Jews entered Palestine, mainly from Poland

and central Europe, and by 1939 the Jews numbered
429,605 out of an estimated population of 1,500,000, i.e. 28
per cent.[20] The fact that it was events in Europe for which
the Arabs were in no way responsible which ultimately
ensured the Zionist control of Palestine added greatly to the
Arab sense of injustice. It was further increased by the
knowledge that other western Christian countries contributed so little to saving European Jewry before 1939.

In December 1935 the British again offered a form of
representative government, through a legislative council on
which the Arabs would have fourteen seats and the Jews
eight.[21] While some of the Arabs would have accepted the
proposal, although they would not have been represented
in proportion to their numbers, the Zionists fiercely rejected
it because it would have given the Arabs a permanent constitutional majority. In April 1936 the various Arab political
parties united sufficiently to form an Arab higher committee under the leadership of Hajj Amin al-Husseini, the
Grand Mufti of Jerusalem. They called for a general strike,
which developed into a general Arab rebellion supported by
Syrian and Iraqi volunteers.

In 1937 a new commission of enquiry under Lord Peel
declared the mandate unworkable and recommended the
creation of an Arab and a Jewish state in Palestine with a
third small state under British administration for Jerusalem,
Bethlehem, Nazareth and the surrounding areas. This idea
was rejected by both Arabs and Jews, and in the following
year was declared unworkable by the Woodhead technical
commission.[22] In 1938 the civil war was renewed with increased violence. A Round Table conference held in London
in the spring of 1939 acknowledged the Arab world's interest
in Palestine by inviting the independent states of Egypt,
Iraq, Saudi Arabia, Transjordan and Yemen to attend, but
it broke down in failure. In May 1939 the British Government, anxious to reduce Arab hostility during the expected
war with Germany, issued a statement of policy in a White

Paper which was anathema to the Zionists.[23] This provided
for the limitation of Zionist immigration to 75,000 over the
next five years with further independence for Palestine after
ten years when further immigration could be decided by the
majority, that is to say the Arabs. Although the Arabs officially rejected the White Paper on the advice of the extremist Hajj Amin, they generally welcomed it and the Arab
rebellion died down for the duration of the war.

In contrast the Zionists were even more determined to
pursue their aim of establishing their own state in Palestine.
Already the Jewish community in Palestine was largely self-
governing through an elected representative assembly which
levied its own taxes. Purely Jewish trade unions were united
in a confederation, the Histadruth, which performed
numerous other functions as banker, entrepreneur and
landowner. Between 1922 and 1939 Jewish colonies had
increased from 47 to 200 and Jewish landholdings from
148,500 acres to 383,350 acres. The most significant development for the future was the creation of the Haganah,
the secret but officially tolerated Jewish army. This gained
experience in defending Jewish settlements against Arab
attacks; some of its members assisted British forces in suppressing the Arab rebellion. The British White Paper turned
the Zionist movement emphatically against Britain for the
first time, but the outbreak of war in September 1939 placed
the Zionists in the paradoxical position of having to support
Britain against the common enemy of Nazi Germany.

British policy in Palestine was beset by the contradictions
implicit in the terms of the peace settlement following the
First World War. British officials in Palestine were divided:
some were pro-Arab, some pro-Zionist, while others tried
vainly to seek a solution which would satisfy both sides. In
general this meant protecting the Arab community against
Zionist ambitions and economic power.

The tranquillity of Transjordan in the inter-war years
was in striking contrast to the turmoil of Palestine. The

British mandate over Palestine included Transjordan, but Article 25 of the mandate, against strong Zionist objections, specifically exempted Transjordan from the operation of the Balfour Declaration. The country was poor, undeveloped and thinly populated, but it enjoyed a social cohesion which Palestine lacked. On 23 May 1923 it was declared an independent state, subject to British obligations under the mandate, and on 20 February 1928 an agreement was concluded by which the Amir Abdullah was to be guided by British advice through a British Resident appointed by the High Commissioner for Palestine (who was also High Commissioner for Transjordan) in such matters as foreign relations, finance and fiscal policy, jurisdiction over foreigners, and freedom of conscience. The 1928 Treaty was supplemented in 1934 by an agreement enabling the Amir to appoint consular representatives in other Arab states, and in 1939 the British government agreed to the formation of a council of ministers in charge of government departments and responsible to the Amir. In 1946 Transjordan became formally independent although remaining heavily dependent on British subsidy and support. The army (known as the Arab Legion), which had a British Commander and a handful of senior British officers, was the most effective of the small armies of the independent Arab states.

6 The Second World War

The outbreak of the Second World War meant that once again the interests of the small and militarily insignificant Middle East countries were relegated to the background. The Great Powers, who were engaged in a mortal struggle, were not concerned with Arab national aspirations except to the very limited extent that they favoured or hindered their war effort. Turkey, the only Middle Eastern state which was both fully independent and militarily significant, belied the hopes of Britain and France by remaining neutral.

Although the 1939 White Paper did much to reduce anti-British hostility among the Arabs, there were some who hoped for an Axis victory. This was much less out of any sympathy with Nazi doctrine and anti-semitism than the belief that it would liberate them from Anglo-French tutelage.

In Syria and Lebanon the situation was confused by the collapse of France in 1940. Some Arab leaders in both countries turned openly towards Germany, but most of them preferred to wait and see the outcome of the war. The submission of all the French forces in the Levant to Vichy caused concern to the British, who declared on 1 July 1940 that they would not tolerate a German occupation of Syria and Lebanon, and imposed a naval blockade which caused severe shortages. The French High Commissioner, General Dentz, tried to conciliate the nationalists, who were demanding the relaxation of French control, but the negotiations broke down.

A crisis was reached in May 1941 as a result of a pro-Axis coup in Iraq. The Vichy Government allowed Germany the use of Syrian airfields to help the Iraqi rebels, and as soon as the revolt collapsed Britain, declaring that Marshal Pétain had betrayed his undertaking not to act against his former allies, invaded Syria and Lebanon with a mixed force of British and Free French troops. Fighting from 8 June to 14 July 1941 was severe; Damascus was spared, but Beirut was severely damaged. An armistice was signed on 14 July which gave French troops and civilians the choice of repatriation or joining the Free French.[1]

As the Allied forces entered Syria and Lebanon on 8 June General de Gaulle's representative, General Catroux, had issued a declaration to the Syrians and Lebanese announcing he had come to put an end to the mandate and to proclaim them 'free and independent'.[2] The British government supported this announcement. However it soon became apparent that de Gaulle had every intention of perpetuating what he himself termed France's dominant and privileged position in the Levant. He instructed Catroux to open negotiations on the basis of the 1936 treaties. A critical struggle ensued in both countries. In Lebanon some Christian elements were prepared to accept a continuation of French rule, but the Muslims and a substantial number of Christians (who together formed a clear majority in the country) were now seeking full independence. Britain, seeing the wider advantages of attracting Arab sympathies in the war (which was going badly for the Allies in 1942), gave its support to the majority.

A crisis was reached in October 1943 when the Lebanese Prime Minister, Riyadh Sulh, announced a programme, which became known as the 'Charter of Independence', in which the constitution was amended to annul most of the mandatory's remaining powers. It also provided for especially close co-operation with the other Arab states if they would respect Lebanese sovereignty and independence. This doctrine, which was subscribed to by all Lebanese Muslim and Christian leaders, was known as the National Pact, and became the corner-stone of Lebanese political life.

The French Committee of Liberation in Algiers rejected the Lebanese demands, and, when the Lebanese parliament proceeded all the same to amend the constitution, the French delegate, General Helleu, ordered the arrest of the President, Prime Minister and three ministers. This provoked a national uprising. Britain intervened to deliver an ultimatum to General Helleu which said that unless the arrested men were released they would be set free by British troops. The French gave way, the President and cabinet were restored to office, and the constitution remained amended. During 1944 most of France's powers were handed over to the Syrian and Lebanese governments. But the crises had not been finally resolved because control of the security forces, or Troupes Spéciales, remained in French hands. France hoped to use these as a bargaining counter to compel the Syrian and Lebanese governments to sign treaties.

Elections in Syria in July 1943 resulted in an overwhelming victory for the nationalists, who demanded the immediate ending of the mandate and rejected France's proposals for a treaty. The situation remained in deadlock throughout 1944, but Syrian and Lebanese resistance to French demands stiffened during 1944. The independence of the two countries had been recognised by several powers, including Britain and the Soviet Union, and in October 1944 the signing of the protocol of Alexandria gave birth to the League of Arab States under British auspices.

When the French landed Senegalese troops at Beirut in May 1945 tension increased sharply in Syria and Lebanon. Similar forces had been used by the French to crush Syrian independence in 1920. Serious disorders broke out in several

Syrian cities and spread to Damascus. The French responded by bombarding the Syrian capital for the second and last time during their mandate. Once again Britain intervened; on this occasion with strong support from the United States government. An ultimatum forced the French troops to cease fire and withdraw to their barracks.

Meanwhile the newly created United Nations provided an ideal platform for the Syrians and Lebanese to present their case. Reluctantly the French gave way under international pressure. In July 1945 it was agreed that Syria and Lebanon should have national armies and the Troupes Spéciales would be handed over to their control. British and French forces were finally withdrawn from both countries in the summer of 1946.

French stubbornness and lack of realism contributed to France's débâcle in Syria and Lebanon. The attitude of Britain and the United States also played a part, but it would in any case have been impossible to restore France's pre-war position in the Levant. French culture was so deeply rooted in Lebanon that it remained powerful after the French departed, but in Syria it was largely submerged by the political antagonism aroused by France's conduct of the mandate.

Iraq had achieved independence in 1932, but the Second World War showed the extent that it remained under British control. Stimulated by Axis propaganda, many nationalist groups were hoping for an Allied defeat in the war. Pro-Axis feeling was strengthened by the presence of the Mufti of Jerusalem, who sought political refuge in Baghdad in October 1939; hostility towards Britain was increased by events in Palestine. But Nuri Said and the royal family remained steadfastly pro-British and in September 1939 Iraq broke off diplomatic relations with Germany. In March 1940 Nuri Said resigned and gave way to an aristocratic Iraqi nationalist, Rashid Ali Gailani—a manoeuvre to make Rashid Ali share responsibility for unpopular pro-British policies.

Supported by four leading army officers, known as the 'Golden Square', Rashid Ali moved Iraq cautiously towards a neutral position in the war. He ordered weapons from Italy and Japan that Britain could not supply. Although the war was going badly for Britain the Iraqi government did not yet dare to denounce the Anglo-Iraqi treaty without guaranteed German support. In November 1940 the British government announced publicly that the Prime Minister of Iraq no longer enjoyed its confidence and began to exert pressure for his resignation. Iraqi resistance hardened and in April 1941 the Golden Square carried out a coup to enforce Rashid Ali's restoration to office. The Regent and Nuri Said escaped to Transjordan.

When the Rashid Ali cabinet refused to allow the landing of British troops in Basra Britain decided to intervene, on the ground that this contravened the Anglo-Iraqi Treaty of 1930. Despite the superficially strong position of the Iraqi army *vis-à-vis* the small British forces in Iraq, Britain succeeded in reversing the situation and overthrowing the Rashid Ali régime with little difficulty. A small force crossed the desert from Transjordan, and another from India was landed at Basra. Iraqi morale was low, opinion was divided, and the promised German aid arrived too late and in too small quantities. Hitler was preoccupied with preparations for invading the Soviet Union.

The Rashid Ali government fled and the Regent and Nuri Said returned. Succeeding Iraqi governments co-operated effectively with the Allies, and Iraq became a base for operations against Iran and for aid to the Soviet Union. In January 1943 Iraq declared war on the Axis powers. But the feelings which had given rise to the Rashid Ali revolt did not disappear. Many Iraqis of later generations were to regard him and his military colleagues as heroes of Iraq's struggle for independence.

Having secured the base in Iraq Britain was able to undertake operations against Iran. At the outbreak of the war Riza Shah had declared his neutrality, but pro-German feeling in the country was strong and the German legation extremely active. Britain feared the threat to its oil supplies, which became more severe as German forces attacked Russia and advanced into the Caucasus in the summer of 1941. Anglo-Russian pressure on Riza Shah to expel all German nationals increased (with the discreet support of the United States which was still officially neutral). With the twin objectives of securing the oil fields and a safe supply line for Russia as an alternative to the vulnerable northern route through Archangel, British and Russian forces entered Iran on 26 August 1941. Iranian resistance ceased after two days and on 16 September Riza Shah abdicated in favour of his twenty-three-year-old son Mohammed Riza. The Iranian government broke off relations with the Axis powers and in September 1943 declared war on Germany.

In a tripartite treaty of alliance in January 1942 Britain and the Soviet Union undertook 'to respect the territorial integrity, sovereignty and political independence of Iran'.[3] They were allowed to maintain armed forces on Iranian soil, but their presence was not to constitute a military occupation and they were to be withdrawn not later than six months after the end of the war. Respect for Iran's independence and sovereignty was confirmed by the Roosevelt, Stalin and Churchill meeting in Tehran in December 1943.

The provision of American war supplies to Russia through the Persian corridor brought some 30,000 non-combatant American troops under British command into Iran by the end of the war. Despite the disclaimer of the tripartite treaty Iran was effectively under military occupation for the duration of the war with the Russians in the northern half of the country and the Anglo-Americans in the southern half. In the face of economic dislocation, inflation and increasing

Soviet interference, the Iranian government had recourse to American civilian advisers and a military mission. This aroused strong Soviet suspicions, and Iran became one of the first battlegrounds in the Cold War before the defeat of Germany.

The hopes that the Anglo-Egyptian Treaty of 1936 might provide a satisfactory basis for relations between the two countries were soon disappointed. The outbreak of war in September 1939 caused Britain to invoke Article VIII which, in placing all Egypt's facilities at its disposal, implied the virtual reoccupation of the country. The Prime Minister declared a state of siege, which amounted to the imposition of martial law with himself as military governor. Egypt did not declare war on Germany. A few leading politicians were in favour, but the majority were opposed, either because they felt it was not Egypt's war or because they were far from certain the Allies would win. On the other hand, Egypt more than fulfilled its obligations under the treaty. German nationals in Egypt were interned and German property placed under sequestration.

Reasonable harmony in Anglo-Egyptian relations was shattered by Italy's entry into the war in May 1940, which brought the fighting into the Middle East and North Africa. Egyptian neutrality suited Britain because of the advantage of Axis acceptance of Cairo as an open city, but a dispute arose over the reluctance of King Farouk and the Prime Minister, Ali Maher, to take action against Italian firms and nationals in Egypt. The King was not especially pro-Axis although he had many Italians in his entourage; Ali Maher was known to have contact with the Italians in North Africa.

The King gave way over Ali Maher's premiership, but his relations with the overbearing British Ambassador, Sir Miles Lampson, which had never been good, deteriorated further. Lampson had strong backing from the British Prime Minister, Churchill, who regarded it as intolerable that the activities of enemy agents in Egypt should jeopardise the Allied war effort in North Africa.

Churchill insisted that Egyptian troops should be withdrawn from the Western Desert to Cairo and that the pro-Axis Egyptian Chief of Staff, General Aziz al-Masri should be dismissed.

Britain wanted to see a Wafdist government under Nahas Pasha installed for the duration of the war. Britain's relations with the Wafd had taken a full turn. The Wafd was ready to co-operate with Britain, and the British government realised that the Wafd, as the popular party, would provide effective support for the Allies.

A crisis was reached in February 1942 when it became known that the King intended to install a palace government led by Ali Maher or one of his friends. Britain regarded the situation as extremely serious; the Axis forces under Rommel had entered Egypt and were advancing towards Alexandria. An ultimatum was delivered to Farouk requiring him either to send for Nahas or to abdicate, and when the King delayed in replying, Sir Miles Lampson, accompanied by an armed force which surrounded the Abdia Palace, forced his way into the King's presence and demanded an immediate decision.

The King gave way and a Wafdist government ensured that the Egyptian home front was made safe for the Allies. The British had secured their immediate objective, but it is arguable that in doing so they had destroyed the monarchy, the Wafd and ultimately their own position in Egypt. The King was losing his early popularity with the Egyptians, but he remained head of state and his humiliation was an affront to the nation. The Wafd's crumbling position deteriorated further as it came to power behind British tanks, and the rising generation of Egyptian nationalists turned increasingly to the Muslim Brotherhood and other militant extra-parliamentary groups. In the army the nascent Free Officers' movement led by Gamal Abdul

Nasser began to lay plans for the overthrow of the monarchy and Egypt's parliamentary system as an essential step towards ending the British occupation.

Palestine was relatively quiet for the duration of the Second World War. The Arab rebellion had died down, and Jewish immigration inevitably slowed to a trickle as Jews were prevented from leaving Nazi-occupied Europe. In the early stages of the war the Zionists in Palestine co-operated with the British, despite the latter's enforcement of the provisions of the White Paper, in the hope of being able to form a Jewish army to fight Nazism. In spite of Churchill's sympathy, the Zionists failed to achieve their object because of British military opposition, although in September 1944 a Jewish brigade group was formed. But the Zionists turned increasingly against Britain as the war progressed. In 1944 a series of attacks by two extremist groups, the Sternists and Irgun, culminated in the assassination of Lord Moyne, the British Minister of State in Cairo. Palestinian Jewry greatly strengthened itself militarily during the war. Apart from the 27,000 who received training in the British forces, the Jewish munitions industry developed rapidly and the unofficial Zionist forces ended the war well supplied with light arms.[4]

Meanwhile international Zionism had shifted its main effort from Britain to the United States, where it gained the support of both major political parties.

The Second World War affected the western Islamic world in many of the same ways as the first. The main fighting occurred in North Africa, rather than in the Levant and Mesopotamia as in the First World War, but in both cases Arabs and Persians were passive spectators or at most minor auxiliaries to the armies of the Powers which fought across their territory. In Iran, Iraq and Egypt the Allies had enforced the installation of sympathetic régimes. The Syrians and Lebanese had benefited from the war by securing their independence, but this was partly because they had been able to win the support of Britain and the United States against France.

By the end of the Second World War the United States had become decisively involved in Middle Eastern affairs, having briefly entered the scene and withdrawn after the First World War. American oil interests in the Middle East, held in check by the war, were on the point of rapid expansion; the wartime connection with Iran was to continue, and of equal importance was the American concern with Zionism, which was to affect United States relations with the Arab world for the next thirty years.

Despite the increased American involvement in the Middle East, it was Britain which appeared as the paramount power in the area in 1945. French rivalry had been eliminated in the Levant and it was primarily British arms which had defeated the Axis forces in the area. Britain retained a huge military base in Egypt, and the Middle East Supply Centre in Cairo, the focus of the Allied war effort in the area, had initiated regional economic planning for the whole Middle East. It was with British encouragement and under British auspices that the League of Arab States was formed. A general Arab conference met in Alexandria from September to October 1944, which was attended by representatives of the governments of Egypt, Iraq, Lebanon, Syria, Transjordan, Saudi Arabia and Yemen and by an observer on behalf of the Arabs of Palestine. The Arab League Pact was signed by the seven independent Arab nations on 22 March 1945.[5] But in reality the supremacy of Britain was already in decline. Exhausted by the war, she was on the point of handing over many of her responsibilities to the United States. At the same time the advent to power of a Labour government in July 1945, with the intention of granting independence to India, meant that a major reason for British interest in the Middle East was removed.

NORTH AFRICA

Although France's authority in North Africa (in contrast to the Levant) was apparently fully restored by 1945, the upheavals of the war had transformed the situation. France's defeat in 1940, the subsequent arrival of Anglo-American forces, the creation of the United Nations and the Arab League, and even the anti-colonial views expressed by President Roosevelt and some of his colleagues all helped to stimulate the desire for national independence in the three Arab Maghrib states. The first stirrings of modern nationalist movements had been observed in the 1930s. In Algeria the Parti Populaire Algérien was formed in 1936. In Tunisia a dynamic new nationalist party, the Neo-Destour, was formed under the leadership of Habib Bourguiba in 1934. He was held in French prisons from 1938 until 1942, when he was released by the Germans. In Morocco in the same year the foundations were laid of co-operation between the nationalists and the young Sultan Muhammad V.

In 1943 the Algerian leader, Ferhat Abbas, formerly an advocate of Algeria's assimilation to France who held that no Algerian nation had existed in history, presented to the French and Allied authorities in North Africa a manifesto embodying Algerian claims. In 1944 France extended French citizenship to certain categories of Muslims, and in 1946 a law granted them fifteen deputies in the National Assembly and seven senators in the Council of the Republic. But any manifestations of Algerian nationalism were harshly suppressed. Algerian soldiers had played an important part in the liberation of France; in 1945 a demonstration at Setif, carrying Algerian flags on the occasion of the Allied victory in Europe, was broken up by the police. A rising followed in which about 100 Europeans were killed. In the course of French reprisals about 10,000 Muslim villagers were massacred.[6]

In Tunisia Bourguiba had refused to collaborate with the Germans, but when French rule was reimposed after the Allied victory his offers of co-operation were rejected by the French authorities; he escaped to Cairo where he set out to gain world support for Tunisian independence.

In Morocco in November 1944 a manifesto signed by members of the National Party and independents called upon the Sultan to begin negotiations with France for the abrogation of the Protectorate Treaty and the recognition of Moroccan independence. The arrest of leading nationalists caused serious unrest. In a speech in Tangier in 1947 the Sultan made himself the spokesman for Moroccan nationalism by claiming Morocco's affiliation with the Arab world and demanding that its legitimate national aspirations be satisfied.

In all three Maghrib states France still seriously underestimated the nationalist challenge. One reason was that in all three countries there were many powerful elements among the Muslim population, including intellectuals as well as landowners, who, either out of self-interest or conviction, remained loyal and refused to consider the possibility of political separation from France.

Yet it was inevitable that nationalist demands should increase. Modern hygiene, introduced by the French, produced an enormous growth in the population. Industry, apart from mining and building, remained rudimentary and the rapidly expanding population was underemployed. Vast *bidonvilles*, or shanty-towns, grew on the outskirts of the major cities, and such industry as there was developed on the basis of an abundant supply of cheap but inefficient labour. In all three Maghrib states the non-Arab inhabitants enjoyed socially and economically privileged positions. In Algeria the number of French settlers had already reached one million by 1930. They were strongly opposed to equality of opportunity for the Algerian Muslims, and the development of higher education was primarily for the benefit of

French or French-speaking students. If the French *colons* thought about the future at all, they saw Algeria, Tunisia and Morocco developing into neo-French states in which French language and culture would remain dominant. The indigenous population could sense that this would mean a permanently subordinate position for all of them except for a small élite who were willing to adopt French culture as their own and abandon their status as Muslims.

Libya had been pacified with some difficulty by the Italians during the 1920s, and in the 1930s substantial colonies of peasant families were settled in Tripolitania and Cyrenaica. Italian policy closely resembled that of the French in North Africa : colonisation and Italianisation. None of the Ottoman state schools survived and many of the local Muslim religious schools were abolished. Secondary education for native Arab children did not exist.

When the Italian forces were finally swept out of the country in 1942 a British Military Administration was set up but Libya's political future had still to be settled. In 1945 the four Powers were unable to agree. The United States favoured U.N. trusteeship, the U.S.S.R. surprisingly asked for the trusteeship of Tripolitania for herself, while France favoured the return of all the Italian colonies to Italy. This was opposed by Britain, which had pledged to Sayyid Idris, head of the Senussi tribe, which had supported the Allies in the war, that they would never be returned to Italian rule. Italy pressed hard its claims to Tripolitania, which were strongly opposed by the Arab states in the U.N. In default of agreement, a majority of the U.N. eventually voted in favour of an independent and united Libya. This was proclaimed in December 1951 with Idris as King.

7 Post-War Unsettlement

If the war had been fought with the inhabitants of the Middle East as passive spectators, it had strengthened their desire to end their satellite status to the western Powers. It was the onset of the Cold War between West and East which prevented the attainment of this objective.

Iran was the scene of one of the first incidents in the Cold War, which had its origins well before the final defeat of Germany. In 1943–4 British and American oil companies and the Soviet Union were all seeking oil concessions in Iran. The Iranian government suspended all oil negotiations until the war was over, but in 1945 the Soviet Union delayed withdrawing its troops from Iran in accordance with the terms of the Tripartite Alliance of 1942, as a means of pressure on the Iranian government. British and American forces had already been withdrawn. The Soviet Union also supported the Iranian communist Tudeh Party in setting up an autonomous socialist republic in Azarbayjan on the Soviet–Iranian border.

In April 1946 the Iranian government reached an oil agreement with the Soviet Union, subject to ratification by the Majlis, and the Soviet troops withdrew in May. The government succeeded in restoring its authority in Azarbayjan and delayed ratification of the Soviet–Iranian oil agreement.

The Cold War began in earnest with the enunciation of the Truman Doctrine set forth in the U.S. President's address to Congress on 12 March 1947, in which he asked for authority to furnish aid to Greece and Turkey (which

Britain was no longer in a position to give) to help them to maintain their integrity and independence against the un-named, but clearly designated Soviet threat.[1] In October 1947 the Truman Doctrine was extended to Iran, and two weeks later the Majlis rejected the Soviet–Iranian oil agreement. In the face of extreme Soviet hostility, the American involvement in Iran increased.

With the Soviet withdrawal the forces of Iranian nationalism were turned against the West and especially Britain, which still monopolised Iranian oil resources. Dr Mohammed Mossadegh, the leading nationalist politician, argued that since Iran had wisely rejected a policy of 'positive balance', which would have implied granting an oil concession to the Soviets to match the British concession in the south, it should pursue a policy of negative balance which implied having no foreign concessions of any kind.[2]

When negotiations for revision of Iran's royalty terms broke down, the nationalist majority in the Majlis passed laws nationalising the oil industry in April 1951, and a month later Dr Mossadegh became Prime Minister. The A.I.O.C. withdrew from Iran and the major international oil companies successfully imposed a boycott on Iranian oil. Britain resorted to economic pressures and military threats, and appealed to the International Court of Justice, which ruled against it, and to the U.N. Security Council, which refused to intervene. The U.S. government attempted unsuccessfully to mediate.

Iran's action aroused responsive enthusiasm throughout the Middle East where the overwhelming military and economic power of the West was deeply resented. Ultimately Mossadegh's revolution failed both because of the strength of the forces opposing him and because of his own inadequacy as a revolutionary leader. In many respects his social and political outlook was reactionary. He opposed the breaking up of large estates in favour of peasant proprietors and he stopped the Shah's land-distribution scheme. He did issue some decrees reducing the landlords' share of agricultural production and abolishing certain feudal dues and services, but since the reforms were to be carried out by committees most of whose members were nominees of the landlords, the results were negligible. In 1952 he took full powers into his own hands; the Shah challenged his actions and had to flee the country in August 1953. However, six days later the Shah returned and overthrew Mossadegh in a counter-coup which is generally believed to have been planned and organised by the American C.I.A.

In Iraq the British troops left by the end of the war, to be followed by most of the rest of the corps of British advisers. Only the more recently recruited technicians and specialists remained. But Britain's influence remained strong since she continued to provide the bulk of economic, technical and military aid, although the United States also undertook an increasing share of this role. The pro-western trend of the Iraqi government aroused increasing opposition from the rising generation of nationalists—university students, the younger army officers and professional men—who were convinced that the country was still governed from the British Embassy. In 1948 they were effective in causing the repudiation of a new Anglo-Iraqi treaty to replace that of 1930, which had been signed at Portsmouth by the Prime Minister, Salih Jabr, and the British Foreign Secretary, Ernest Bevin. Despite the greatly improved economic prospects due to increasing oil revenues, Iraq was proving as difficult to govern as ever, as new elements of division based on social and economic interests appeared in addition to those based on racial and religious sectarianism.

Britain was equally unsuccessful in placing its relations with Egypt on a new footing. Preoccupied with a number of apparently more pressing matters, the British Labour government at first believed rather vaguely that the 1936 Anglo-Egyptian Treaty would hold with a few modifications. Military opinion still regarded the retention of a major military base in Egypt as a vital necessity. In the face of the incipient, but growing, Soviet threat it was hoped to include Egypt in a regional defence pact. British troops remained in the major Egyptian cities as a constant provocation to Egyptian nationalist opinion.

With a background of anti-British rioting and strikes, the elderly Sidky Pasha, who had been recalled to form a government, reached an agreement with Ernest Bevin in which the Labour government, which had considerably softened its attitude, accepted the principle of total evacuation from Egypt, although still hoping to create a regional defence organisation to replace the Suez base. The accord was denounced as a sell-out by the Conservative opposition, but once again agreement foundered on the Sudanese problem. Vague diplomatic wording led Sidky Pasha to believe that Britain had accepted Egyptian–Sudanese unity under the Egyptian crown, but Britain had no such intention. British military opinion held that in the event of a withdrawal from Egypt it was even more urgent to retain control of the Sudan. British troops were withdrawn from the delta cities to the Suez Canal zone, but they remained seven times as numerous as the 10,000 stipulated in the 1936 Treaty.

At this time events in Egypt and Iraq were overshadowed by what was happening in Palestine. As soon as the war was over the U.S. President, Truman, formally requested the British government to allow the immediate immigration of 100,000 Jews to Palestine, while the U.S. Congress called for unrestricted Jewish immigration to the limit of the country's economic absorptive capacity. The British Foreign Secretary, although angered at the U.S. intervention, which he considered made a complex problem more difficult, decided to secure American co-responsibility by setting up an Anglo-American Commission of Enquiry. In its report in April 1946 the Commission recommended the continuation of the mandate and the immediate admission of 100,000 Jewish immigrants, but criticised the continued existence of

Jewish underground forces, estimated at 65,000.[3] President Truman at once pressed for the immediate admission of the 100,000, but the British government insisted on the prior disbandment of the Jewish irregulars. The mandate government now had to deal with illegal immigration on a massive scale and a widespread Zionist campaign of terrorism, which culminated in the blowing up of the King David's Hotel in Jerusalem and the British government and military offices which it housed, in July 1946.

Meanwhile the Arab states were attempting to mobilise their diplomatic and military forces on behalf of the Palestinian Arabs through the newly-founded Arab League. But their political and military weakness as well as their internal divisions were apparent.

In 1947 Britain finally abandoned hope of reconciling the conflict of interests. It was under strong economic and political pressure from the United States on behalf of the Zionists, but was unwilling to endanger any further its relations with the Arab states. It therefore decided to hand over the whole problem to the United Nations. A U.N. Special Committee on Palestine (U.N.S.C.O.P.) recommended in a majority report the partition of Palestine into Arab and Jewish states, with Jerusalem and its environs to remain under international control. Partition was adopted by the U.N. General Assembly on 29 November 1947 by a vote of 33 to 13, with 10 abstentions.[4] The favourable vote was secured by strong U.S. pressure on a number of smaller nations; the Soviet Union also voted in favour of the resolution. All the Islamic Asian countries voted against, and an Arab proposal to ask the International Court of Justice to judge the competence of the General Assembly to partition a country against the wishes of a majority of its inhabitants was only narrowly defeated.

The Arabs totally rejected partition, but the Zionists accepted it; the resolution provided for a Jewish state including 55 per cent of Palestine at a time when Jews formed

30 per cent of the population owning less than 8 per cent of the land area.[5] U.N.S.C.O.P. had intended that Britain should supervise the implementation of partition, but Britain refused because it was not acceptable to both sides. It announced that it would be relinquishing its mandate for Palestine on 15 May 1948.

The U.N. partition resolution touched off violent Arab protests which soon developed into communal fighting. Armed volunteers arrived from Syria to help the Arabs, but in general they were no match for the more cohesive, better trained and armed Zionists. Arab villagers, terrified by reports of events such as the massacre of the inhabitants of Deir Yasin by Irgunists, left their homes *en masse*. Haifa fell to the Zionists on 22 April and Jaffa on 13 May.

On 14 May 1948 the last British troops left with the High Commissioner, and on the same day the Zionists proclaimed the state of Israel, which was promptly recognised by the United States (in accordance with a prior undertaking by President Truman) and by the Soviet Union. Early on 15 May units of the regular armies of Syria, Transjordan, Iraq and Egypt entered Palestine in support of the Palestinian Arabs. They scored some initial successes and the Egyptians linked up with the Arab Legion near Bethlehem, but the Israelis, fighting desperately in the knowledge that their survival depended on the outcome, launched a violent counter-offensive, which ended in an Arab collapse. The overwhelming Arab superiority in numbers was not reflected on the battlefield, where the total of Arab regular forces engaged was 21,500 compared with an estimated 65,000 Jewish troops. The Zionists were better equipped, and they secured important fresh arms supplies from Czechoslovakia while fighting was in progress.

In spite of the efforts of the United Nations, fighting did not finally stop until January 1949, and the conclusion of armistice agreements between Israel on the one hand, and Egypt, Syria, Transjordan and Lebanon on the other, was

not completed until July. Israel now comprised nearly 80
per cent of the area of the Palestine mandate, and the
number of Arabs within the area of Israel had diminished
from between 700,000 and 750,000 to 165,000.[6] Of the 21
per cent of Palestine which remained in Arab hands, the
desert Gaza Strip was placed under Egyptian administration, and the substantial enclave on the West Bank of the
Jordan, which included the old city of Jerusalem, was annexed by Transjordan in 1950 against strong opposition
from the other Arab states, following elections on both sides
of the river.

The Palestine war and the harsh injustices to the indigenous inhabitants left a legacy of bitterness among all
the Arabs against Israel and against the two western Powers
most responsible for its creation—Britain and the United
States. It has been the single most powerful factor behind
the radicalisation of the Arab world and the growth of anti-
western feeling over the past two decades. The deep sense of
grievance has been kept alive by the presence in neighbouring Arab states of Palestinian Arab refugees, swollen in
numbers by the 1967 six-day war and natural increase to
about 1·5 million in 1972. A U.N. General Assembly resolution of 11 December 1948,[7] affirming their right to a
choice of repatriation or compensation, has remained a dead
letter, although reaffirmed almost every year, since Israel
insists that it must be part of a general settlement.

Angry and humiliated, the Arabs made it clear that they
had no intention of accepting Israel. In November 1950 the
Arab League decided to continue the war-time blockade of
Israel on the ground that an armistice did not constitute a
state of peace. One direct consequence of the war was to
jeopardise the position of the substantial Jewish communities in several Arab states. As the Zionists urged their
emigration to the new state of Israel they became the
object of suspicion to Arab Governments. Five-sixths of
Iraq's 150,000 Jews left for Israel in the next few years.

The social and political repercussions of the disaster were felt in most parts of the Arab world. In Syria the discredited parliamentary régime was overthrown by a bloodless military coup in March 1949 led by Colonel Husni Zaim. Two further coups took place before the end of the year, and, although constitutional life was resumed in 1950, the Syrian Army's intervention in politics, whether directly or indirectly, was to become permanent.[8]

The effects on Egypt of the Palestine war were equally profound although they took longer to mature. The King and Nahas Pasha were both determined that Egypt should lead the Arab unity movement, but the Prime Minister, Nokrashy Pasha, who was fully aware of the Egyptian Army's weakness, had grave misgivings about Egypt's involvement. The corruption and inefficiency with which the Egyptian expeditionary force was organised convinced the younger officers more than ever of the criminal incompetence of their rulers. King Farouk did not improve his image by divorcing his popular Egyptian wife when the war was at its height.

In the aftermath of the war acts of terrorism, mostly by the Muslim Brotherhood, rapidly increased as did acts of counter-terrorism by the secret police. The standard of public life deteriorated from its previous low level. After an improbable last minute reconciliation between King Farouk and Nahas Pasha, the Wafd returned to power with its usual sweeping victory, which this time was to be its last. British hopes that this would lead to an improvement in Anglo-Egyptian relations were soon disappointed as the Wafd discovered that its only means of restoring its declining popularity was to show hostility towards Britain. The British government proposed a plan for a combined Middle East command with the U.S., Turkey and France, as well as Britain and Egypt, in the same week of October 1951[9] that the Wafd decided on the desperate course of unilaterally abrogating the Anglo-Egyptian Treaty of 1936. The

Egyptian government not only cut off fresh food supplies and withdrew Egyptian labour from the British Suez Canal base, but encouraged the formation of volunteer 'Liberation' squads to carry out sabotage and guerrilla attacks. These were successful in rendering the base militarily useless, as the 80,000 British troops became wholly absorbed in protecting themselves and their families. British military opinion began to revise its views of the necessity of retaining the base. But it was a highly dangerous course for the Wafd because it meant further encouragement for the increasingly powerful anti-constitutional forces in the country.

British counteraction against guerrilla attacks led inevitably to a major incident. On 25 January a British force surrounded the Ismailia police headquarters and gave it an ultimatum to surrender. The post resisted on the orders of the Minister of the Interior and some fifty Egyptian police were killed. The following day a frenzied Cairo mob, led by the Muslim Brothers and other militant groups, burned the centre of Cairo, concentrating their attacks on British property and buildings with foreign associations. The regular army delayed intervening to restore order until the evening.

The incident hastened the end of the Egyptian monarchy and parliamentary régime. As one helpless government succeeded another, the Free Officers' organisation decided to act, and six months later, in an almost bloodless coup, they seized power and sent King Farouk into exile.

8　The Rise of Nasserism

THE 1952 Revolution was not only a milestone in Egypt's long history, but was also to exert a powerful influence on the Arab world and many of the emerging nations of the Third World.

Egypt was now ruled by true native Egyptians for the first time in over 2000 years. Their triple objective in seizing power was to overthrow the monarchy, to secure a British evacuation and to reform the social and political system by eliminating the power of the landowning classes. Above all they aimed at restoring sovereignty to the Egyptian people.

That the overthrow of the monarchy and parliamentary constitution was much more than a mere military coup was due largely to the qualities of thirty-four-year-old Colonel Gamal Abdul Nasser, the creator of the Free Officers' movement, who was to wield near absolute control over Egypt domestic and foreign policies for most of the two following decades. A few of the Free Officers leaned towards Marxism or the Islamic reformism of the Muslim Brotherhood, but Nasser, like the majority, had no coherent political ideology at this stage. The body of ideas and practice which became known as Arab socialism was developed pragmatically over the years.

One major act of social and political reform was carried out immediately after the 1952 Revolution. Less than half of one per cent of the landowners between them owned over one-third of all cultivable land in Egypt, while 72 per cent of cultivators owned less than one feddan (1·038 acre)

each, amounting to only 13 per cent of the land. The
agrarian reform limited all land holdings to 200 feddans
(with an extra 100 if the owner had two or more children)
and redistributed the confiscated land to 'fellahin' (that is
to say Egyptian peasants) in lots of two to five feddans. The
reform decree also sharply reduced the rents that it was legal
for landowners to charge their tenants.[1]

The reform was radical rather than revolutionary or
Marxist. Alone it was certainly incapable of solving Egypt's
agrarian problems, although, because it was generally successful in avoiding disastrous falls in agricultural output, it
served as a model for other developing countries. It did
succeed in its prime objective of reducing the overwhelming
political powers of the big landowners who had successfully
blocked social and political reforms for generations.

Apart from the symbolic abolition of the Ottoman titles
of Bey and Pasha and the banning of political parties, land
reform was the only important domestic innovation of the
early years of the Revolution. From 1952 to 1954 Nasser was
heavily absorbed in a struggle for power with Muhammad
Naguib and the Muslim Brothers, and in securing a British
evacuation.

Naguib had not been one of the Free Officers, but had
been brought in to head their committee a few months
before the Revolution because they needed someone of his
rank and reputation as their figurehead. After the Revolution he had automatically become President of the Revolutionary Command Council (R.C.C.). But Naguib, although
honest and popular, was far from being a natural revolutionary leader. Conservative in temperament, he felt his
office entitled him to exercise authority over the hot-headed
young officers in the R.C.C. He was also politically naïve;
he was outmanoeuvred by Nasser who soon revealed himself
as a masterly political tactician. Naguib allowed himself to
be placed in a position of advocating a return to the pre-

revolutionary political system, which was something that the army in particular would not tolerate.

The military régime had little difficulty in eliminating the hollow and discredited political parties. The principal challenge came from the Muslim Brothers and the communists. Of the two the Brotherhood, with its nationwide organisation, was much the more formidable and, having played a leading role in undermining the monarchy, it felt it was entitled to at least a share of power in the new régime. The Brotherhood's tendency to violence was its undoing. An assassination attempt on Nasser by one of the Brothers in October 1954 provided grounds for suppressing their organisation, and because it was proved that Naguib had connections with the Brotherhood, although it was never suggested that he was implicated in the assassination attempt, he was removed from office and placed under house arrest.

By the end of 1954 Nasser was in undisputed control of Egypt. His freedom of manoeuvre was greatly enhanced by the settlement of the two outstanding political questions which had beset Egypt for over fifty years—the British military occupation and the Sudan. Failure to settle the latter had long prevented a solution of the former and the R.C.C.'s decision to separate the two questions went half way towards a solution. The Sudan problem was tackled first, and an Anglo-Egyptian agreement for immediate Sudanese autonomy followed by self-determination after three years was reached on 12 February 1953.[2] In a sense both parties were bluffing. Neither was able to reject the principle of Sudanisation and self-government when the other proposed it. The Egyptians hoped and expected that an independent Sudan would opt for union with Egypt. The British were counting on Sudanese elections resulting in a pro-British (and anti-Egyptian) régime under the conservative Umma party. They were shocked when the pro-Egyptian parties won the elections, but the R.C.C. was equally taken aback when the new Sudanese government of

Ismail al-Azhari decided on complete independence and against union with Egypt. Sudanese independence was declared on 1 January 1956.

The R.C.C. was bitterly disappointed over the Sudan, but the agreement made it possible to begin the vital negotiations over the British Suez base. Talks continued intermittently throughout 1953 and early 1954. A basic obstacle to the agreement was that Britain still regarded Egypt as a western Protectorate, but it was made easier by the fact that Egypt was no longer the centre of British Middle East policy. Turkey had joined NATO in the autumn of 1952, and the British joint armed forces H.Q. was moved from Suez to Cyprus in December. The United States, which was quite favourably disposed to the new Egyptian régime, was also strongly urging Britain towards a settlement.

Nasser stood firm in rejecting a British demand to keep 7000 servicemen in Suez, but he agreed to the reactivation of the base in the event of an outside attack on any Arab states or Turkey. As the negotiations dragged on, he allowed guerrilla attacks on the base area to be resumed as a means of pressure on Britain. Finally agreement was reached in July 1954 on the basis of a British proposal to evacuate all British troops and maintain the base on a seven-year lease with a cadre of civilians on contract to British firms.[3] In accordance with the agreement the last British troops left Egypt on 31 March 1956. After seventy-four years Egypt was free of foreign occupation.

Although there was some criticism in Egypt of the compromise terms of the agreement, Nasser's prestige in the Arab world was rapidly growing. He had already shown awareness of the kind of role that Egypt could play in his little book, *Philosophy of the Revolution*, published in 1954, where he spoke of its location at the coincidence of three circles—the Arab Circle, the African Circle and the Islamic Circle. As the biggest, and in some ways the most developed, Arab state, Egypt's qualifications for Arab leadership were obvious, however detached from the Arab world it had been in the past. In Africa the struggle of the emergent black nations for independence was only just beginning. Nasser remarked, 'Surely the people of Africa will continue to look to us—we who are the guardians of the continent's north-eastern gate and constitute the link between Africa and the outside world.' Similarly, Cairo with its ancient Islamic university of al-Azhar was certain to be a major focal point in the Muslim world.

New horizons were opened for Nasser in 1955. In April he attended the Afro-Asian Conference at Bandung in Indonesia where the importance of Egypt and its revolution was acknowledged as he was treated as an equal by Asian statesmen such as Nehru, Chou En-lai and Sukarno. Already his friendship with Nehru and Tito of Yugoslavia was helping to form his ideas of the advantages of neutralism or non-alignment with the Great Power blocs. In the case of Egypt, which so long had been regarded by the West as part of its sphere of influence, neutralism meant strengthening its ties with the Soviet Union and the communist bloc. Except for its Iranian intervention in 1945 the Soviet Union had not regarded itself as a Middle Eastern power, and it played virtually no role in the Arab world where it was regarded with suspicion for having favoured the creation of Israel. But following the death of Stalin in March 1953 the Soviets began to adopt a more flexible and adventurous Middle East policy. Instead of lending support to the small and uninfluential communist parties in the Arab states the Soviets turned towards backing popular national leaders who were prepared to show independence from the West. Nasser was this type of Arab leader *par excellence*.

The two inevitable consequences of this development in Egypt's foreign policy were that its relations with the western Powers should deteriorate, and that Israel should begin to regard Nasser's Egypt as its principal external challenge. The hostility towards Nasser of Britain's Eden government had originated with the frequently acrimonious negotiations over the Sudan and the Suez Base. The Anglo-Egyptian Agreement had manifestly failed to improve relations between the two countries. In 1955 their mutual hostility greatly increased with the conclusion of a series of military agreements between Iraq, Turkey, Pakistan, Iran and Britain, which became known as the Baghdad Pact.[5] The idea of this anti-Soviet alliance had originated with the United States, which had dropped it on realising that the Arabs were much more concerned with Israel than with any Soviet threat. But Britain had joined as a means of maintaining some part of its dominant position in the area. Nasser tried every means to prevent Iraq from joining because he saw the Pact, with its NATO links through Turkey, as an instrument of continued western domination, but he failed to persuade the indefatigably pro-western and anti-Soviet Nuri Said.

The great mass of articulate Arab opinion was on Nasser's side in this matter. His influence was enough to prevent Jordan from joining. But, as Nasser's popularity with the Arabs grew, the hostility he aroused in the West increased.

When Nasser came to power he had every reason to avoid involvement with Israel. He was not only confronted by major domestic and foreign problems requiring solution, but the Palestine war had exposed the weakness of the Egyptian armed forces. The Israeli premiership of the moderate Moshe Sharett from December 1953 to February 1955 was a period of relative Egyptian–Israeli *détente*, but in that month the scandal of the Lavon affair—the failure of a plan by the Israeli Secret Service to force the British to stay in Egypt by simulating Egyptian outrages against British institutions—brought the militant activist David Ben Gurion back to power in Israel on 21 February 1955. One week later Israel resumed its policy of heavy reprisal for incursions by armed Palestinians with a massive raid on Gaza, which destroyed the Egyptian headquarters and inflicted heavy casualties.

This event was a turning-point in modern Middle Eastern history.[6] It exposed Egypt's military weakness and provoked demands for retaliation from the Egyptians which Nasser could not ignore. He now began to look for a major source of arms supplies. Because the West was refusing to supply more than small quantities on onerous financial terms he turned to the Soviets who responded favourably. In September 1955 Nasser announced an agreement to purchase large quantities of Soviet arms via Czechoslovakia—the first deal of its kind by any Arab country.

Western hostility towards Nasser reached new heights. France had joined the ranks of his enemies, mainly because it was convinced that the Algerian rebellion which had broken out in 1954 was stimulated and financed from Cairo. A Franco-Israeli alliance which was to last for more than a decade was formed, and news of a secret deal to supply Israel with French weapons had added to the urgency of Nasser's search for arms. British antagonism had reached a point where the Eden government was convinced that Nasser's aim was to destroy all of Britain's remaining interests in the Arab world. He was held responsible for every manifestation of Arab anti-western feeling, including Jordan's sudden dismissal of the British Commander-in-Chief of the Arab Legion, General Glubb. Moreover, Egypt had begun to play the role in the African Circle that Nasser predicted. Cairo had become a centre for anti-colonial liberation movements throughout Africa, and Egyptian Radio gave vigorous support in numerous African languages. The United States, with fewer direct interests in the Middle East than Britain or France, was chiefly concerned with the Cold War aspect of Nasser's neutralism. Pro-Zionist Congressmen reinforced the chorus of those who were saying that Nasser's aim was to unite the Arab states by force and turn them into Soviet satellites.

But the western Powers had not altogether abandoned hope of keeping Egypt within their orbit. The new Egyptian régime had set its heart on the building of a giant dam on the Nile near Aswan, which by increasing the cultivated area by thirty per cent and enormously increasing its hydro-electric supply, would form the corner-stone of Egypt's development programme. In February 1956 a provisional agreement was reached whereby the World Bank would loan $200 million on condition that the United States and Britain loaned another $70 million to pay the hard currency costs. The U.S. and Britain imposed conditions which Nasser found hard to accept since they involved some western control over the Egyptian economy. When he finally made up his mind to accept the U.S. and Britain had already decided to withdraw the offer. The U.S. Secretary of State, John Foster Dulles, abruptly announced that the offer was being withdrawn because the Egyptian economy was too unstable for so large a scheme. Anti-Egyptian opinion in the U.S. had hardened in May when Nasser suddenly recognised Communist China. It is possible that the U.S. and Britain never seriously expected the Dam to be built, but it is certain that they did not foresee Nasser's reaction, or that the Soviet Union would replace the West in providing aid for the Dam.

One week later, on 26 July 1956, Nasser announced that the Suez Canal Company ('our Canal') was nationalised, and the profits would be used to finance the High Dam. Not only Arabs but people throughout the Third World were thrilled by this daring challenge to the western colonial powers. It was dangerous because Britain and France were determined to use force if necessary to wrest the Canal from Egypt's control. Egypt's strength lay in the fact that the United States, while strongly disapproving of the nationalisation, was opposed to the use of force. This was also the view of most other users of the Canal. The Soviet Union expressed full support for Egypt's action.

During three months of abortive negotiations a Franco-Israeli plan for Israel to invade Sinai with French support was extended to include Britain. Israel invaded Sinai on 29 October and two days later British and French planes began to bomb Egyptian air fields. On 5 November British and French troops landed in the Port Said area.

The Arab world was in uproar as hostility to Britain and France reached fever pitch. World opinion was also over-whelmingly hostile towards the Anglo-French-Israeli action, and, after the creation of a U.N. Emergency Force (U.N.E.F.),[7] Britain and France were obliged to withdraw.

The threatened break-up of the British Commonwealth, Soviet warnings, and especially the opposition of the United States, which refused to provide aid to relieve the alarming drain on sterling, all contributed to Britain's decision to halt its Suez action. Britain and France also made two major miscalculations about Egypt : one was that the Egyptians would be incapable of managing the Canal on their own, and the other that as soon as hostilities had begun there would be a popular uprising against Nasser. In fact the Egyptians managed the Canal very efficiently, and Nasser's popularity in Egypt and the Arab world reached new heights. Militarily Egypt had been defeated by over-whelming power, but its political gains were substantial. The Suez Canal base, with its huge quantities of stores, was taken over by Egypt, and the still considerable British and French economic interests in Egypt were nationalised. The relics of the Anglo-French dual control of Egypt were eliminated.

The Suez affair gave new impetus to the underlying anti-western radical trend in the Arab countries. The sympathy gained by the United States among the Arabs for its role in halting the Anglo-French action and in pressurising a reluctant Israel to withdraw from Sinai and Gaza was only very temporary. The Eisenhower–Dulles administration was still guided by Cold War principles. It rapidly mended its bridges with Britain, France and Israel and initiated a campaign to reinforce the remaining conservative pro-western elements in the Arab world and to contain the rising tide of Nasserism. This involved joining the western economic blockade of Egypt which made it even more heavily dependent on the Soviet Union, and promoting what came to be called the Eisenhower Doctrine : the offer of military and financial aid to any Middle East countries 'requesting such aid against overt aggression from any nation controlled by international communism'. The consequence was greatly to increase the ideological ferment in the Arab world and to strengthen the alliance between the Soviet Union and radical Arab nationalism.

But the overwhelming popular appeal of Nasserism among the Arab masses was causing anxiety in some areas of the Arab world. In addition to Nuri Said in Iraq, the established rulers of most of the independent Arab states were basically pro-western and conservative. They regarded the rising power of Nasserism, aided by Cairo's immensely powerful radio and press propaganda as well as ubiquitous Egyptian agents, as a deadly threat. Encouraged by the United States, these anti-Nasser forces began to show their hand in 1957.

The major oil-producing states of the Middle East—Iraq, Saudi Arabia and Kuwait—had gained substantial increases in revenues in the 1950s, as a result of the introduction of the principle of fifty–fifty profit sharing between the oil companies and the governments of the producing states to replace the old system of royalty payment per ton.* But the

* Iran lost its position as the leading Middle East oil producer as a result of the nationalisation dispute. However, after the fall of Mossadegh a new concession was negotiated with British, American, French and Dutch oil interests, known collectively as the Consortium. This provided generous compensation for British Petroleum (formerly A.I.O.C.). Iran's oil revenues began to recover but *per capita* they remained well below those of the other Middle East states.

increased wealth did not necessarily make the régimes in these countries stronger or more stable; if anything, social tensions were increased, and Egyptian propaganda lost no opportunity to point out the glaring inequalities of wealth they were causing. Kuwait was the most fortunate because with its tiny population (about 200,000) its paternalistic but relatively enlightened régime was able to ensure rapidly improved living standards for all its population.

King Ibn Saud died in November 1953. His patriarchal bedouin type of administration was quite unable to cope with the new flood of wealth. His son Saud, who succeeded him, was a man of inferior qualities, whose ludicrous extravagances made him the laughing-stock of the Arab world and cast doubts on the future of the Saudi monarchy. In Iraq the oil wealth was much more wisely used. In 1950 a Development Board was established and was allocated seventy per cent of the rapidly increasing revenues, although it never received the full amount. As investments were made in the economic infrastructure, flood control and irrigation, and Iraq's great economic potential began to be realised, the living standards of the mass of the population started to rise slowly from their low levels. But the lack of any social policy, and the investment in long-term projects rather than education and social services (which would have brought speedier and more easily appreciable benefits to the majority), combined with the fact that many of the development projects merely increased the wealth of the large landowners, tended to encourage the radical and revolutionary forces in the country.

Syria, although lacking in oil, was also a country of high potential. But its post-independence economic boom based on investment in the new cotton industry had slowed down by the mid-1950s, and the country was acquiring a worldwide reputation for the chronic instability of its régimes. The fall of the dictator, Colonel Adib Shishakly, who ruled Syria fairly effectively from 1950 to 1954, brought a return to constitutional government with a parliament apparently dominated by the traditional political parties. But the really significant trend was the growing power of the minority Baath (renaissance) Socialist Party. The Baath had been founded in 1943 by two Damascus school teachers, Michel Aflaq, a Christian who was the party ideologist, and Silah Bitar, the organiser. It emerged as an officially constituted political movement after the departure of the French in 1946, and in 1952 it gained in strength by a union with the Socialist Party of Akram Hourani, a politician with an important following in central Syria.

The ideas of Michel Aflaq, a withdrawn ascetic who has been called the 'Gandhi of Arab nationalism', are idealistic and at times almost mystical. They owe something to Marxism and to romantic nineteenth-century German nationalism, but he gave them a specifically Arab character. He summarised the three Arab objectives as 'Freedom, Unity and Socialism' and his central slogan was 'One Arab Nation with an Eternal Mission'. Freedom meant political, cultural and religious liberty as well as liberation from colonial rule. Unity meant not only the political unification of the Arab peoples, but their regeneration through the release of the 'hidden vitality' which is the true source of nationalism. Baathist socialism was based less on socio-economic principles than on a rather vague ideal of national moral improvement, and neither Aflaq nor Bitar showed much interest in the adoption of specific socialist measures. All they said was that socialism was a means of abolishing poverty, ignorance and disease, and achieving progress towards an advanced industrial society capable of dealing on equal terms with other nations.[8]

In its bid for radical or progressive leadership in the Arab world the advantage of Baathism was that, in contrast to Nasserism, it was not attached to any individual leader or Arab state. Significant Baathist movements developed during the 1950s in Lebanon, Jordan and Iraq, as well as

Syria. Its disadvantage was its failure to win mass support, so that when Baathists succeeded in gaining power they were unable to hold it except by extreme dictatorial or fascist-type methods.

Jordan was the most vulnerable of all the Arab states as its very existence were constantly called into question. Over half its population were Palestinians and, although they had accepted the union with Transjordan out of necessity, most of them felt no loyalty or sympathy towards their new Hashemite rulers. On 20 July 1951 King Abdullah was assassinated in Jerusalem by a Palestinian*, and was succeeded by his son Talal, who one year later was declared mentally unstable. Talal's seventeen-year-old son Hussein inherited the formidable task of ruling the turbulent kingdom. His position was not made any easier by the heavy Israeli reprisal raids on Jordanian frontier villages in response to infiltration attacks by dispossessed Palestinian farmers. Hussein attempted to preserve Jordan's ties with the West, but these came increasingly under attack from nationalist elements, who received the support of Egypt, Syria and Saudi Arabia. King Saud was no radical nationalist, but he opposed the Hashemites and the Baghdad Pact for dynastic reasons. Hussein earned some respite by his dismissal of General Glubb, the British Commander-in-Chief of the Jordanian Army in March 1956, but anti-western feeling in Jordan was inflamed by the Suez affair. The pro-Nasser nationalist government in October 1956 terminated the agreement with Britain, and in January 1957 Egypt, Saudi Arabia and Syria signed the Arab Solidarity Agreement by which they undertook to make annual payments to Jordan in place of the British subsidy. All British troops were withdrawn from Jordan by the summer of 1957.

The tide in the Arab world was flowing strongly in Nasser's direction, but during 1957 his opponents rallied.

* The Husseini family of the Mufti of Jerusalem were implicated in the plot.

In April King Hussein carried out a coup against his own pro-Nasser Government, which had aimed to establish diplomatic relations with the Soviet Union. The King had two strong assets in defending his throne : the loyal support of the bedouin elements of the East Bank, who are pre-dominant in the Jordanian Army, and the very real fear that in the event of his overthrow Israel would occupy the West Bank up to the River Jordan.

King Saud of Saudi Arabia, becoming increasingly appre-hensive about the republican trend of Arab nationalism, sent troops to help King Hussein. In Lebanon the majority of the Christian half of the population and not a few of the Muslims followed the lead of the able and ambitious President Chamoun in openly displaying pro-western sympathies.

The whole Middle East was becoming increasingly divided along Cold War lines into two mutually hostile camps. The unconcealed efforts of the United States and Britain to set up a pro-western front against Nasser in-creased tension and gave added force to Soviet propaganda. Not for the last time, both the Soviet Union and the U.S. were particularly concerned with developments in Syria, which Mr Dulles feared was about to become a Soviet satellite. His fears were exaggerated because, although the anti-western trend in Syria was very real and the communist party, although small, was the most formidable in the Arab world, the great majority of Syrians had no intention of becoming part of the Soviet system. They were equally in no mood to accept the Eisenhower Doctrine; instead the Baathists, who held the key posts in the government, led the country into asking Nasser to form an immediate and comprehensive union between Syria and Egypt. This was proclaimed in February 1958 and called the United Arab Republic.

From then on events moved rapidly. In March 1958 King Saud was forced to relinquish his powers to his brother

Prince Feisal after the Syrians had accused the King of plotting to assassinate Nasser and so prevent the Syrian-Egyptian union. At the time Feisal was regarded as more pro-Egyptian and less pro-western than his brother the King.

In Lebanon in May the dangerous division caused by the Suez crisis developed into a muted civil war which simmered on throughout the summer, with Syria, now part of the United Arab Republic, aiding and encouraging the nationalist rebellion against President Chamoun and his pro-western government.

The climax came with the Iraqi Revolution of 14 July 1958. It was Nuri Said's decision to help Chamoun which led to his downfall. Brigadier-General Abdul Karim Kassem and his subordinate officer Colonel Abdul Salam Aref had been ordered in early July to proceed with their troops to Jordan. Almost certainly the plan was to invade Syria and destroy the union with Egypt. Instead Kassem and Aref seized power in Baghdad; Nuri Said, the young King, and his uncle the Crown Prince, were assassinated and an Iraqi Republic declared. At one blow the strongest and most effective pro-western bastion in the Arab world had fallen. Fearing that what remained of their interest in the area would be overwhelmed, the U.S. answered Chamoun's urgent request by landing marines in Lebanon and Britain flew troops into Jordan to help protect King Hussein. But there could be no question of a western military counter-offensive against triumphant Nasserism. In Lebanon the civil war was ended with a compromise by the election of the moderate General Chehab, Commander-in-Chief of the army, as president, and the formation of a government with leaders from both sides in the dispute. Lebanon's independence had been preserved, but its foreign policy reverted to being less overtly pro-western and more acceptable to Arab nationalists.

Nasser and Nasserism were at the height of their success.

Not only was Egypt in control of the heartland of Arab nationalism in Syria, but its principal rival in Iraq had been destroyed. Even the elderly and ultra-reactionary Imam Ahmad of Yemen attempted to insure his own future by applying to join the union; a loose federal structure known as the United Arab States was formed of Yemen and the U.A.R. It was not apparent to many at the time, but Nasserism had reached a peak from which some decline was inevitable. In reality Nasser's extraordinary successes—which were partly due to the mistakes of his opponents and their failure to understand the true nature of his appeal to the Arab masses—had concealed the underlying weakness in his position. Suez and its aftermath had given Egypt an international status which it could not hope to sustain. Although Nasser himself was aware of the many practical obstacles to the achievement of a political union of the Arab states and to the liberation of Palestine from the Zionists, his many Arab followers now regarded him as a hero—a new Saladin who would unite the Arab peoples and defeat the invaders. On occasions his own intoxicating rhetoric seemed to minimise the difficulties.

It was not long before his triumphant progress received a severe setback. First the new Iraqi-Egyptian entente was short-lived as General Kassem had Colonel Aref, who publicly favoured an immediate Iraqi-Egyptian union, arrested and imprisoned. Kassem blamed an abortive revolt in Mosul in February 1959 on Nasser. During 1959 the Iraqi communists strengthened their position at the expense of Arab unionists, and Nasser became convinced they presented a serious threat to the whole Arab nation. Kassem managed to survive in power for nearly four years by playing off one side against the other, but Nasser distrusted and bitterly attacked him. Kassem, a vain and unstable man, developed a violent and jealous hatred of Nasser in return.

Nasser's criticisms of the Iraqi communists led to a serious break with the Soviet Union, and jeopardised Soviet military and financial aid to Egypt (including the High Dam). This had the advantage of demonstrating convincingly that Nasser was genuinely non-aligned and unsubservient to the Soviets. It also led to a partial rapprochement with the U.S., a resumption of American aid to Egypt and some improvement in relations with Jordan and Saudi Arabia, but the failure of the two leading progressive or revolutionary Arab states to form an effective alliance was a bitter disappointment to most Arabs.

Nasser's rule in Syria was even more crucial because this was the first practical test of Arab political unity. When the Syrians had first asked for the union Nasser hesitated saying he preferred a transitional period of five years. When he did consent it was on his own terms; the union would be a complete merger and heavily centralised. All political parties must be dissolved.

The Baathists had provided the Syrian initiative for the union, and expected to rule Syria under the umbrella of Nasser's prestige. But Nasser had no intention of allowing the Baath a monopoly of control. In October 1959 he appointed Abdul Hakim Amer, his closest associate, as virtual governor of Syria, and in December the Baathist ministers in the U.A.R. Government resigned to go into opposition or sullen self-exile. As the government of the U.A.R. became increasingly centralised in Cairo, all the factions and interests which had cause to resent the union tended to coalesce : politicians whose parties had been dissolved, merchants, landowners and businessmen who disliked the application of Egyptian socialist legislation to Syria, army officers and civil servants who found Egyptians placed over them. In general the Syrians, who regarded themselves as the forerunners of Arab nationalism, felt they were relegated to a subordinate position to Egypt. On 28 September 1961 the disaffected elements in Syria struck. A group of army officers revolted and soon had the country in their hands.[9] Nasser at first thought of intervening but he soon realised that coercion was hopeless. It was now the turn of Nasser's enemies in Jordan, Iraq and Saudi Arabia to triumph. King Hussein recognised the new Syrian régime within hours.

Having decided to make the best of a bad business Nasser announced that it was not imperative for Syria to remain part of the U.A.R., and he would not oppose its re-entry as a separate nation into the U.N. or the Arab League. Egypt, however, would remain the United Arab Republic.

Nasser acted with courage and composure, but there was no denying he had suffered a heavy setback. Some thought that he might fall from power, others that he would turn away from the Arab world to concentrate on Egypt's domestic problems. He now had the opportunity to do this because, according to his testimony, the task of ruling Syria absorbed three-quarters of his time. There was a serious need for him to devote attention to the development of Egypt's political structure, which his preoccupation with foreign affairs had caused him to neglect.

When the Free Officers came to power they had no ideology except a simple nationalist anti-colonialism and no developed political and economic ideas. Apart from agrarian reform, which was primarily political in its aims, the R.C.C.'s economic policies were initially cautious and conservative. In the mid-1950s there had been some progress towards the rather vague concept of a 'socialist, democratic, co-operative' society, but it was still gradual. Nasser and his colleagues were becoming aware that if they were to achieve the rapid industrialisation, the high economic growth rates, the expansion of the social services and the building of the High Dam, which alone would satisfy the popular expectations raised by the 1952 Revolution, they must mobilise all Egypt's human and economic resources. Inevitably this led to an increase in the role of the public sector. The trend was greatly accelerated by the Suez affair, which placed all the substantial British and French economic interests in the hands of the state and strengthened Egypt's ties with the communist countries.[10]

By 1960 the Egyptian régime had finally abandoned its earlier belief that industrialisation could be achieved by the private sector under the general supervision of the state. A series of decrees in the summer of 1961 took the U.A.R. a long way towards socialism by nationalising cotton export firms, banks and insurance companies, and either wholly or partly nationalising 275 major industrial and trading companies, sharply increasing income tax and reducing the maximum land-holding from 200 to 100 feddans. (It was the application of these decrees to the Syrian region of the U.A.R. which caused the Syrian bourgeoisie to support the break-up of the union.)

But with all this very little had been done to create a workable political system in Egypt. Under the 1956 constitution Nasser had become President and the R.C.C. was abolished. A single political organisation, the National Union, had been established as a substitute for political parties to which Nasser was as always implacably opposed. But the National Union had proved unsatisfactory. It had failed to take root and its complex constitution was little understood by the Egyptian masses.[11] Moreover Nasser was convinced that the Syrian right wing had managed to infiltrate it in order to launch its coup against the union. Convinced that the Egyptian bourgeoisie might be planning similar action, he launched a precautionary counter-offensive in which the property of most of Egypt's wealthiest families was sequestered. (The fact that Egypt still had multi-millionaires was an indication that the socialist re-distribution of wealth had not progressed very far.)

In May 1962 a National Congress of Popular Powers, attended by labour unions, professional associations and other community groups, met in Cairo to debate the Charter of National Action which Nasser had been preparing during the winter. The 30,000-word Charter went some way towards defining Nasser's idea of Arab socialism. Starting from the proposition that parliamentary democracy as practised in Egypt after the First World War was 'a shameful farce', its essence was contained in the passage which declared :

Political democracy cannot be separated from social democracy. No citizen can be regarded as free to vote unless he is given the following three guarantees : (a) he should be free from exploitation in all its forms; (b) he should enjoy an equal opportunity with his fellow citizens to enjoy a fair share of the national wealth; (c) his mind should be free from all anxiety likely to undermine his future security.[12]

In accordance with these principles the Charter said that most of the economy should be publicly owned—that is, all railways, roads, ports, airports and other public services, banks and insurance companies and the majority of heavy, medium, and mining industries. All the import trade and three-quarters of the export trade must be controlled by the public sector, which within the coming eight years must also take charge of at least one-quarter of domestic trade to prevent monopoly; ownership of agricultural land was limited to 100 feddans per family (but there was no question of land nationalisation). Private ownership of buildings was maintained with constant supervision to prevent exploitation.[13]

The new and unique political organisation was to be known as the Arab Socialist Union—a pyramidal organisation founded on the 'basic units' in villages, factories, and workshops and rising through elected councils at the district and governorate levels to the National Executive headed by the President. The legislative branch of the A.S.U. was the National Assembly. In this, as in all the elected bodies of the A.S.U., half the seats had to be formed by workers or farmers (defined as anyone owning less than twenty-five feddans).[14] By this means Nasser hoped to ensure greater participation in government by the masses. Other important principles of the Charter referred to the need for female equality and family planning.[15] It specifically recognised the need to raise the social levels of the countryside to those of the towns.

The National Congress approved the Charter without amendment. In September 1962 Nasser restored cabinet government with Ali Sabri as Prime Minister.

9 North Africa Wins Independence

TUNISIA

FRANCE'S attempt to reimpose the full authority of its protectorate over Tunisia after the Second World War met with vigorous opposition from the nationalist Neo-Destour Party and other independent groups who demanded autonomy and the formation of a Tunisian parliament. The more liberal approach of the new Resident-General failed to satisfy these demands, and in 1950 the French government decided to offer Tunisia internal autonomy to be achieved by negotiated stages. A Tunisian government was formed with the Neo-Destour Secretary-General, Salah ben Youssef, as a member. The government negotiated some increase in its powers at the expense of French control and the reform of civil service regulations to give priority to the recruitment of Tunisians. But the powerful French colony in Tunisia (about 180,000) opposed the extension of autonomy and succeeded in influencing the Paris government to block further reforms. A new Resident-General adopted a hard line; he arrested Bourguiba (who had just returned to Tunisia from Egypt) and other senior members of the Neo-Destour, although Salah ben Youssef succeeded in escaping to Cairo. Growing agitation led to acts of terrorism against French police and Tunisians who collaborated with the French. The French resorted to counter-terrorism, and organised bands of fighters or *fellaghas* appeared in the mountains.

In July 1954 an important conciliatory step was taken by

the French government of Pierre Mendès-France, which recognised Tunisia's right to full autonomy, and proposed the immediate opening of negotiations for a convention to confirm the new status and regulate French interests in Tunisia. A Tunisian government was formed with the participation of a large number of Neo-Destour ministers, and lengthy negotiations, which were still obstructed by the opposition of the French colony in Tunisia, ended with the signing of the Franco-Tunisian Conventions in June 1955.[1] Habib Bourguiba returned from France to a massive popular welcome.

Three months later Salah ben Youssef returned from Egypt to lead a violent campaign from the left against Bourguiba and the Franco-Tunisian Conventions. Bourguiba won the struggle because he enjoyed the support of the Neo-Destour; Salah ben Youssef fled the country.

The Conventions still placed severe limitations on Tunisian sovereignty. It was, therefore, inevitable that when Morocco gained a promise of full independence from France in November 1955, Bourguiba should ask for the same for Tunisia. This was finally granted by the Socialist government of Guy Mollet and proclaimed in a protocol in March 1956.[2] It was left to later negotiations to establish the basis of Franco-Tunisian interdependence to replace the 1955 Conventions.

Bourguiba formed a new government entirely from Neo-Destour personalities. The Bey of Tunis had become no more than a figurehead. In July 1957 Bourguiba abolished the monarchy and became President of the Tunisian Republic, as well as Prime Minister.

Franco-Tunisian relations were far from settled because of the continuing war in Algeria. While French troops remained stationed in Tunisia, the Algerian rebels were using Tunisia as a base and refuge. A severe crisis in February 1959, caused by the French bombing of a Tunisian village, was settled through Anglo-American mediation. The French

President, de Gaulle, agreed to the withdrawal of all French troops except for the garrison of Bizerta, which remained under French control pending a final settlement. Failure to solve this issue caused Bourguiba to press his claim with force in 1961 and violent fighting led to the loss of 1000 Tunisian lives. The Bizerta base was eventually handed over to Tunisia in December 1963.

MOROCCO

Sultan Muhammad V became the natural focus for the Moroccan national movement following the Second World War. General Juin, who was appointed Resident-General in 1957, exerted pressure on the Sultan to disassociate himself from the *Istiqlal* (independence) party but without success, although the French were able to draw on their supporters among the *Caids* or feudal leaders of the countryside as a counterweight to the more nationalistic towns. In the early 1950s the national movement spread and consolidated itself even among the tribes. It began to receive support from the Arab League, the Afro-Asian bloc in the U.N. and a section of French opinion. However a majority of the French Moroccan colony was in favour of repression and they enjoyed powerful influence in Paris. In 1953 a group of pro-French Caids (some of whom had personal grievances against the Sultan) demanded the deposition of Muhammad V. After deposing and deporting him, the French authorities replaced him with an elderly cousin, Sidi ben Arafa, who could be relied upon to cause no trouble. As a result Muhammad V became an even more potent symbol of the national spirit.[3]

A clandestine organisation replaced the banned political party and launched a terrorist campaign. After several assassination attempts against him the new Sultan ceased to appear in public. The French took severe reprisals, but

one by one the Moroccan opponents of Muhammad V re
versed their position and rallied to his cause. By 1955 th
French had no alternative but to bring back the depose
Sultan. By the Declaration of La Celle St Cloud of
November 1955 France agreed to terminate the Protectorat
and recognise the independence of Morocco. In retur
Morocco recognised French interests and accepted 'inde
pendence within interdependence', which were to be define
by freely negotiated agreements. These were completed b
2 March 1956 and a full transfer of power was made.
similar arrangement was made with the Spanish govern
ment for the incorporation of the Spanish zone with th
independent kingdom of Morocco.

ALGERIA

France's willingness to concede independence to Tunisi
and Morocco was partly motivated by its desire to retai
its third North African territory to which it was most closel
attached—Algeria. Various proposals for assimilatin
Algeria with France, although supported by some leadin
Algerian personalities such as Ferhat Abbas, had failed be
cause France consistently refused to grant Algerians fu
French citizenship with political rights unless they renounce
their personal status as Muslims, which was something tha
the great majority refused to do. The law was relaxed i
1944 to extend French citizenship to certain categories o
Muslims, but they remained a small minority. The incipien
uprising and savage French reprisals of 1945 widened th
gulf between the two communities and finally proved th
impossibility of assimilation. In 1947 a different, thoug
related, formula was proposed, which just conceivably woul
have worked if it had been fully applied. The Statute o
1947 created an elected Algerian Assembly with substantia
autonomous powers. It allowed Algerian Muslims to becom

full French citizens while keeping their Koranic status, reaffirmed the independence of the Muslim religion, and provided for the teaching of Arabic at all educational levels. But, as with the assimilation policy, implications of full integration were never faced.[4] French politicians of all colours affirmed that Algeria was part of France but were not prepared to accept the logical consequence of having 100 Muslim deputies in the French parliament. At the same time the French settler community in Algeria, which was even more influential in Paris than those in Morocco and Tunisia, prevented the application of the principles of social and political equality to the Muslim Algerians.

Despair at the lack of progress caused the Muslims to break out in rebellion on 1 November 1954. The appointment of Jacques Soustelle, who had a liberal reputation, as Governor-General in 1955 seemed to offer a chance for a fresh start.[5] But it was too late. As the rebellion spread and French reprisals aimed at 'pacification' became more severe, all plans for political reforms were rendered futile. Soustelle himself moved towards the right to become the idol of extremist French settlers. During 1956 nearly all the outstanding Muslim political leaders, who had held back when the rebellion began, joined the rebels' political headquarters in Cairo.

The French elections of January 1956 brought to power the Republican Front which had fought the electoral campaign on a platform of 'peace in Algeria'. But the Socialist Prime Minister, Guy Mollet, proved incapable of bringing the war to an end. His policy of trying to suppress the rebellion before holding elections and negotiating with the representatives of the Algerian people was a failure. 'Pacification', which involved the despatch of vast numbers of French soldiers to Algeria (500,000 by the early 1960s), the use of paratroops and the resettlement of some 1,250,000 villagers under the supervision of the army, succeeded in eliminating much of the military strength of the rebellion.

But French severity, which included the use of torture to extract information, only widened the gulf between the two communities, and the revolt continued. In October 1956 the French scored an apparent success when a plane carrying five rebel leaders headed by Ahmad Ben Bella from Morocco, where they had been the guests of the Sultan, to Tunis was diverted to Algeria and the five men were arrested by the French. But the Algerian Revolt was rapidly becoming an international issue. The whole Arab world, which had been further embittered against France by its role in the Suez affair, took up the cause of the Algerians. Despite French objections the subject was discussed at the U.N. from 1957 onwards. Although France could be said to be winning the war militarily, it was losing it politically. The discovery of important oilfields in southern Algeria in early 1957 gave France an added incentive to maintain its hold over the country.

The French colonists (or *pieds noirs*) retained a powerful influence in Paris. In May 1958 their suspicions that the government was preparing to negotiate with the rebels caused them to launch a successful combined assault on the Fourth Republic in alliance with the French right and bring Charles de Gaulle to power. In September 1958 the rebels responded by forming their own government-in-exile headed by Ferhat Abbas.

Although it was not immediately apparent, the high hopes placed on de Gaulle by the French settlers were to be totally deceived. With his exceptional powers under the new constitution the President and government were no longer subject to the French settlers' blackmail. Step by step and deliberately obscuring the path he was taking, de Gaulle moved towards acceptance of the principle of Algerian independence. As the French right became aware of what was happening, the settlers in alliance with some elements in the army came out in revolt twice in 1960 and 1961, but were suppressed. Secret negotiations between the French govern-

ment and the rebels began in 1961 and culminated in the
Evian agreements of March 1962, which laid down the
principles of future Franco-Algerian social and economic
co-operation and provided for a referendum to be held
throughout Algeria on the choice of independence. A terror
campaign against the Evian agreements launched by the
French extremist O.A.S. (Organisation de l'Armée Secrète)
failed in its objective, and in the next six months some
800,000 of the 1,000,000 Europeans in Algeria left the
country. In the referendum held on 1 July the Algerians
voted by a huge majority in favour of independence in co-
operation with France.

The exiled Algerian leaders returned, and a struggle for
power ensued between Ben Khedda (who had succeeded
Ferhat Abbas as head of the provisional government in
1961) and Ben Bella, who won with the support of the
Algerian people's army under Colonel Houari Boumedienne.
The strongly socialist Ben Bella became Prime Minister in
September 1962 and President of the Algerian Republic in
1963.

The Algerians aroused widespread admiration for the
courage and determination of their struggle for independence against apparently overwhelming odds. But the cost
of the eight-year war was devastating when measured by
the hundreds of thousands of military and civilian casualties,
the uprooting of the rural masses, large-scale emigration and
the decline of agriculture.[6] The departure of the European
settlers deprived the country almost entirely of technicians
and professional men. The Algerian Muslims had proved
their existence as a nation, but the problems of independence required as much courage as the struggle which had
achieved it.

10 The Arab World 1962–1972

ALTHOUGH Nasser was able to pay greater attention to domestic affairs after the break-up of the union with Syria, there was never any serious question of Egypt withdrawing entirely from its involvement in the Arab world. Nasserism had suffered a severe set-back, but it remained a powerful influence on the Arab masses (including the Syrians) and was feared by other Arab governments.

In 1962 the leaders of Jordan, Syria, Saudi Arabia and Iraq were all attacking him from different standpoints. The Saudis and Yemenis concentrated mainly on Egyptian socialism, which they said was alien and atheistic. Syria where a series of weak governments followed the secession from the U.A.R., accused Nasser and Egypt of criminally tyrannical behaviour during the Union. At a meeting of the Arab League in Lebanon in August the Syrians listed their complaints against Egypt in the most violent terms. Nasser withdrew his delegates from the meeting and announced that Egypt was leaving the Arab League.

In September 1962 there was an important development when some officers in the Yemeni army revolted against the Imam Badr, who had just succeeded his father the Imam Ahmad, seized the main towns and declared a republic. Badr escaped and with help from members of his family rallied support among the tribes. The Yemeni revolutionaries at once appealed to Nasser for help. Nasser responded with the despatch of an expeditionary force to help defend the Yemeni Republic.

Egypt's involvement in Yemen, which was to last five years, was to prove expensive and difficult. The troops, which Egypt could ill spare, had to be increased at one time to 50,000; they were untrained for the mountain guerrilla warfare in which they were engaged. As the Egyptians became increasingly involved in the administration of the politically fragile republic the cry of 'Egyptian imperialism' was raised by their enemies. Egypt's image was not improved by its attempts at 'pacification' through the bombing of defenceless villages.

Yet at the outset the Yemeni revolt gave back to Nasser the initiative in the Middle East. In showing that his forces were capable of coming to the aid of the Yemenis his stock rose among the Arab masses. The establishment of the first republic on the Arabian peninsula placed the Arab monarchies on the defensive. Both Jordan and Saudi Arabia began to help the Yemeni royalists, but several Jordanian and Saudi air force pilots defected to Cairo.

The establishment of the Yemeni Republic also affected the position in south Arabia—the last remaining territory in the Arab world under British rule. Britain began withdrawing from its paramount position in the Persian Gulf when Kuwait became fully independent in 1961 and the Anglo-Kuwaiti Treaty of 1899 was revoked. Abdul Karim Kassem then promptly claimed Kuwait as part of Iraq. At the request of the Ruler of Kuwait Britain landed troops to defend Kuwait's independence, but these were shortly afterwards replaced, with Kuwait's agreement, by a joint Arab League force. It was apparent that Kuwait's status as an independent state and its acceptance by the international community depended more on the approval of the majority of Arab states than on British military protection.

Britain retained a small military and naval base in Bahrain, but the Aden base was of much greater importance.

It was regarded as the main defence for Britain's considerable economic interests in the Persian Gulf and a vital
strategic link with the Far East. In 1954 Britain began a
policy of persuading the tribal sheikhs and sultans in the
Aden Protectorate to federate.[1] This was actively opposed
by the Imam of Yemen as an infringement of the status quo
agreed to in the Anglo-Yemeni Treaty of 1934. With support from Egypt and other Arab states he began a sabotage
and guerrilla campaign against the neighbouring Protectorate sheikhdoms. Although reluctant to give up their independence, six agreed to federate in 1958. In 1959 Britain
agreed in principle to help the new Federation of South
Arabia towards independence and founded a federal capital
near Aden.[2] By 1962 four more chiefs had agreed to join.

Meanwhile a strong Arab nationalist movement was developing in Aden Colony which with its schools, trade
unions and civil service was considerably more advanced
than the economically backward Protectorate states. Britain
tried to bring the movement under control by repression
combined with limited moves towards self government, but
the British position was made very much more difficult by
the advent of the Yemeni Republic. As the Protectorate
sheikhs, with Britain's tacit approval, gave their support to
the Yemeni royalists fighting the Republic, Egyptian forces
in Yemen gave active assistance to the anti-British nationalist forces in the area. In 1963 British pressure succeeded in
forcing through a merger between Aden Colony and the
Federation of South Arabia against the wishes of the Adeni
nationalists, who feared they would come under the political
control of the tribal sheikhs whom they regarded as feudal
and reactionary.[3] From then on the situation in Aden
steadily deteriorated as assassinations and bombing became
daily occurrences. By the mid-1960s a familiar picture presented itself. The Aden base was rapidly becoming militarily
useless as the British troops were forced to devote their
energies to protecting themselves and their families, while

counter measures against the nationalists increased anti-British feelings.

In 1963 events elsewhere in the Arab world began to move swiftly under pressure from the underlying radical nationalist forces. In February Abdul Karim Kassem was overthrown and shot in a coup led by Baathists and Nasser's friend Abdul Salam Aref was installed as president. A month later the weak Syrian régime also collapsed under joint pressure from Baghdad and Cairo. Here also the Baathists took over in alliance with a variety of Nasserist and Arab unionist groups. Both the new Iraqi and Syrian régimes pledged themselves to support the new movement of Arab unity.

This was another apparent moment of great triumph for Nasser since there were now five of what he termed 'liberated Arab states' sharing similar ideals (U.A.R., Yemen, Syria, Iraq and Algeria), and three of them had agreed to start immediate negotiations for the formation of a federal union.[4] But disillusion came even more swiftly than with the Syrian–Egyptian union as the mutual mistrust between Nasser and the Baathists came to the surface. While the Baathists now saw their opportunity to seize the leadership of the progressive Arab nationalist movement, Nasser was equally determined that they should not. The trilateral union negotiations revealed the bitterness and mistrust and although a form of agreement on a tripartite federation was reached on 17 April the union was stillborn. During May and June the Syrian Baathists were purging the army of non-Baathist officers and suppressing Nasserist demonstrations. Following the ruthless suppression of a pro-Nasser coup in Syria in July Nasser openly attacked the Baath for the first time, revealing that Egyptian intelligence had discovered an Iraqi-Syrian alliance against him.[5]

Egypt's relations with Iraq and Syria now rapidly worsened. Nasser had some satisfaction in November when the Iraqi Baathists, who had already made themselves un-

popular with their violent methods and who had renewe
the exhausting war with the Kurdish nationalist minority
split into right and left wing factions and were ousted b
President Aref, whom they had kept as a figurehead, an
some senior non-Baathist officers. Aref resumed pressure fo
union with Egypt, but although an Iraqi-Egyptian Join
Political Command was created, experience made Nasse
extremely cautious. He suggested to the Iraqis that the
should first ensure their own national unity, which amon
other things meant finding a solution to the Kurdis
problem.[6]

Although Arab political union seemed impossible in th
winter of 1963-4 Nasser saw the urgent need for some kin
of joint Arab action. The Israelis had completed the diver
sion of some of the waters of the River Jordan to the Nege
Desert and this was something the Arabs had sworn t
prevent. The Arab masses expected their governments t
act. In their divided condition there was little hope of thei
taking effective action, but there was a very real danger tha
one Arab state—most probably Syria—would act on its ow
and plunge the others into a war with Israel for which the
were not prepared. Nasser therefore issued an invitation t
all Arab kings and presidents, which he knew they woul
find it difficult to refuse, to meet in Cairo in January 196
to discuss the situation. He made use of the occasion t
mend his bridges with Arab states such as Jordan, Tunisi
and Morocco from which he was estranged and to empha
sise the isolation of Baathist Syria. The heads of state agree
to set up a Unified Arab Military Command under a
Egyptian general and also a Palestine Liberation Organisa
tion (but not a government in exile), with its own army, t
represent the Palestinian people. They all agreed, althoug
with little enthusiasm, on the choice of the flamboyan
Palestinian lawyer, Ahmad Shukairy, to head the P.L.C
They also decided on plans to divert the sources of the Rive

Jordan in Arab territory in order to forestall Israel's irrigation schemes.

The pressing problem of how to satisfy Arab aspirations
for the liberation of Palestine without provoking a poten-
tially disastrous war with Israel had been postponed rather
than solved. The decisions of the kings and presidents gave
the Arabs a false sense that some positive and united action
was at last being undertaken. Lebanon and Syria were reluctant to carry out the diversion work on the Jordan
tributaries in their territory without more adequate protection than the Arab states could provide, and the mutual
trust between Arab governments which was essential if the
U.A.M.C. was to be effective was lacking. During 1965 and
1966 the division deepened between the conservative camp
(led by Saudia Arabia) and the radical camp (led by Egypt).
Although President Nasser and Prince Feisal (the real ruler
of Saudi Arabia since his brother Saud was in bad health)
agreed publicly on the need to settle the Yemeni problem, neither was prepared to make the necessary compromise. There was the added complication that the
progressive camp was divided by hostility between Nasserists
and Baathists.

Nasser continued to play a prominent role on the world
stage. In May 1964 the Soviet Premier Kruschev made a
much publicised visit to Egypt for the inauguration of the
second stage of the building of the High Dam—the gigantic
project which not only aimed to change the face of Egypt
but was the symbol of Soviet aid to the Third World. In July
Nasser was host to the second conference of the Organisation
of African Unity. Although in practice Nasser's 'African
Circle' had not been as important for Egypt as his Arab
Circle, for reasons of language, racial and religious affinity,
and strategic interest, Egypt was undeniably one of the
major states on the African continent. In October 1964
fifty-six heads of non-aligned states or their representatives
met in the U.A.R. capital for a conference. The concept of

non-alignment may have been incapable of precise definition, but it had real meaning to most countries of the Third
World and Nasser was undoubtedly one of its leading advo-
cates.

Nasser's function as a world statesman could not help to
solve his domestic difficulties. Rapid and sometimes ill-
planned policies of industrialisation and economic expansion, combined with a reduction in western aid, had placed
Egypt heavily in debt and destroyed its credit. The discovery of a nation-wide conspiracy by a revived Muslim
Brotherhood revealed a profound ideological and political
dissatisfaction in many levels of society. In August 1965
Nasser made a sudden visit to Jedda in Saudi Arabia to
reach an agreement with King Feisal (who had succeeded
Saud on the latter's abdication in December 1964) on the
Yemen, which provided for Yemeni self-determination and
the ending of all Saudi and Egyptian intervention. The
agreement failed to provide a solution because neither side
trusted the other enough to be wholly sincere. In December
1965 King Feisal went on a state visit to Iran, and in his
address to the Iranian Majlis he suggested the need for
Islamic unity against subversive and alien influence from
outside. Although he was deliberately unspecific, no one
doubted he was referring to Egypt's Arab socialism. The
conservative anti-Nasserist forces in the Middle East rallied
to King Feisal's 'Islamic Front'. Feisal was a much more
formidable statesman than his brother Saud, and rapidly
increasing oil revenues gave his country a new power and
status.

Events were moving rapidly towards the tragic dénoue-
ment of a third Arab–Israeli war. In February 1966 the
Syrian régime, which had begun a rapprochement with
Egypt, was overthrown by the radical wing of the party. The
new rulers of Syria had no love for Nasser, but they were
more strongly hostile towards the Arab kings and, if possible, even more bellicose than their predecessors towards

Israel. The deteriorating situation in the Middle East drew the Egyptians and Syrians closer together. King Hussein of Jordan was trying to prevent Palestinian Arab commandos (*fedayyin*)* from operating from Jordanian territory, and he refused to allow the Palestinian Liberation Army, which was being trained in Gaza, to enter Jordan. But Syria was giving the *fedayyin* encouragement and support, and accordingly Israel's threats of heavy retaliation were principally directed against Syria. In June 1966 Egypt signed a trade and payments agreement with Syria, and in November a comprehensive (and fateful) defensive pact. As always Nasser found it impossible to reject a Syrian appeal for assistance.

A few days later three Israeli soldiers were killed by a mine explosion near the Jordanian frontier.[7] Although Syria was clearly the main source of Palestinian sabotage attacks, Israel launched its customary heavy retaliation raid against the West Bank village of Samua. Protesting against their inadequate protection by the Jordanian army, the West Bank rose in revolt and were only quelled with difficulty. In a bitter speech King Hussein attacked Nasser for his criticisms of Jordan, and taunted him with hiding behind the protection of the U.N.E.F. which had kept the Egyptian–Israeli front quiet since 1956.

Tension rose to a new height the following spring as Israeli leaders issued increasingly severe warning to Syria. Soviet, Syrian and Egyptian intelligence combined to warn Nasser that an Israeli attack on Syria was imminent. Nasser's response on 18 May was to ask the U.N. Secretary-General to withdraw the U.N.E.F. from Sinai (where, on Israel's insistence, it was stationed only on Egypt's side of the border). When U Thant complied the road to war was wide open. Nasser moved a division across the Suez Canal into

---

* *Al-Assifa*, the military wing of the principal Palestinian resistance organisation al-Fatah, issued its first communiqué on 1 January 1965.

Sinai and, with the eyes of the Arab world upon him, ordered the closure of the Straits of Tiran to Israeli shipping. King Hussein, realising that war was now probable and that it would be impossible for Jordan to stand aside, made a dramatic flight to Cairo on 30 May to sign a Jordanian–U.A.R. defence pact.

The Arab countries were now in a state of emotional self-intoxication as a final victory over Israel seemed imminent. Even Nasser seems to have abandoned his usual doubts about Arab military capabilities, although he may have believed that U.S. restraint on Israel would prevent her from attacking, and that he could score a tactical victory without fighting. He himself had promised the Soviets that Egypt would not strike first. However, experience would have told him of the high probability that Israel would attack as soon as it became apparent that the international community was not going to force the Straits of Tiran on Israel's behalf. Any last doubts should have been removed when the activist General Moshe Dayan joined the Israeli cabinet on 1 June.

In a surprise attack on the morning of 5 June Israel destroyed most of the Egyptian air force on the ground. With complete command of the air, Israeli forces won an easy victory in Sinai and reached the Suez Canal early on 9 June. After destroying the Egyptian Air Force Israel could turn against Jordan, which had entered the war as Egypt's ally. By the evening of 7 June, with the Old City of Jerusalem and the East Bank occupied, Jordan accepted the U.N. Security Council's demand for a ceasefire; Egypt accepted on the following day. Israel was now free to turn against Syria, which had confined itself to probing attacks. Israeli troops stormed up the Golan Heights and occupied the key town of Quneitra on the Syrian plateau. Syria accepted the ceasefire on 10 June.[8]

The swift and shattering Arab defeat in the Six-Day War had many immediate and long-term consequences. Nasser's heavy share of responsibility was clear, and on the afternoon

of 9 June he announced his intention of resigning and handing over to Vice-President Zakariya Muhiaddin. The extraordinary dominance which he had achieved in Egypt, and
his position as the generally well-loved father figure of a
nation accustomed to paternalistic rule, meant that he was
not allowed to abandon the presidency at a time of such
desperate crisis. Inevitably his image was damaged, although
not destroyed. His health was deteriorating and there is little
doubt that the disasters of 1967 and their consequences
shortened his life. But in one sense Egypt's difficult situation
made his position easier, since those who might have challenged his power were restrained by their lack of any practical alternative to his policies. In August 1967 he was faced
with a conspiracy to restore his former right-hand man,
Abdul Hakim Amer, as head of the armed forces, and in
1968 and 1969 there were serious outbreaks of student and
industrial unrest, but he overcame these with a mixture of
firmness and mild concessions. While there was considerable
dissatisfaction, especially among the professional classes and
intelligentsia, because the old power structure had not been
radically changed, the continuing state of emergency with
Israel provided a powerful argument for postponing fundamental reforms. Jordan's losses from the war were relatively
greater than Egypt's. Some 150,000 new refugees had fled
across the River Jordan to the East Bank.[9] The closure of
the Suez Canal made Aqaba, the country's only port, virtually useless, and Israel's occupation of East Jerusalem and
the West Bank ruined the flourishing trade. Jordan's survival
as an independent state seemed more than ever in doubt.

An Arab summit meeting in Khartoum in August 1967
agreed on a policy of no peace and no negotiations with
Israel. At the same time the three wealthiest oil-producing
Arab states—Kuwait, Saudi Arabia and Jordan—agreed to
provide Egypt with £90 million a year (and Jordan with
£35 million) to meet the consequences of the war. President
Nasser and King Feisal also reached a bilateral agreement

to wind up their involvement in the Yemeni civil war, and Egyptian troops were all withdrawn by the end of the year.

Soviet aid in repairing Egypt's defences, the Arab contributions, new oil discoveries, the benefits of the High Dam which was now nearing completion, the withdrawal from Yemen, and Egypt's own improved financial management, all helped to shield the country from the worst economic consequences of the war. But the final settlement of the Arab–Israeli dispute which alone would have enabled Egypt to concentrate on solving its social and economic problems seemed a very distant prospect. President Nasser and King Hussein based their foreign policy on the British sponsored U.N. Security Council Resolution 242 of 22 November 1967, which called in precisely defined terms for the withdrawal of Israeli forces 'from territories occupied in the recent conflict' and for respect for the right of all Middle Eastern states 'to live in peace within secure and recognised boundaries'. The weakness of this resolution from Egypt and Jordan's point of view was Israel's contention that its security required the retention of a military presence in all the occupied territories. Israel also maintained its absolute determination to keep a united Jerusalem under its rule. None of the Great Powers, including the United States, accepted Israel's claims. President Nixon's Republican administration, which took office in January 1969, stated explicitly that the pre-June 1967 boundaries should apply except for minor changes. But the United States was not prepared to support the concerted pressure which alone might have forced Israel to relinquish the occupied territories.

Arab pride prevented Egypt and Jordan from negotiating directly with Israel while it remained in occupation of their territory. Moreover the U.N. Resolution 242 did not call for such negotiations. The renewal of full-scale war was impossible because Israel retained overwhelming superiority even if the Arabs were united which they were not.

President Nasser therefore maintained a policy of 'no peace, no war', which was dangerous and unsatisfactory but allowed the postponement of more drastic alternatives. Egyptian probing raids against the Israeli Suez Canal front brought heavy retaliation. The bombardment of the Suez Canal towns necessitated the evacuation of civilians to the interior. Israeli-Egyptian engagements in 1968 and 1969 were not all one-sided, and Israel's monthly casualties were enough to cause concern in Israel, but Egyptian forces in the Canal Zone suffered severely from the massive Israeli bombardment. In August 1970 both sides agreed to the ceasefire proposed by the U.S. Secretary of State as part of a renewed peace initiative. An uneasy calm was restored but the move towards a general settlement ran into the sand.

One striking consequence of the 1967 war was the revival of national consciousness among the Palestinian Arabs. Between 1948 and 1967 the Palestinians had pinned their faith mainly on the Arab states to liberate their lost territory, and most of them had been content to merge their identity into a broad Arab, as opposed to Palestinian, nationalism. Even the use of the name Palestine declined. After the 1967 defeat of the Arab regular armies the Palestinians reached a collective conclusion that the restoration of their country depended on their own efforts. The Palestinian guerrilla organisations, which had appeared on the scene in 1965–6, gathered support and prestige. Arab governments and individuals helped to provide them with arms and funds. Outside the Arab world the cause of Palestine liberation also gained adherents, especially on the left, as many people became aware for the first time of the injustices the Palestinians had suffered.

It was the misfortune of the Palestinians that the enthusiasm they aroused only concealed their military and organisational weakness. The open nature of the terrain in the Israeli-occupied territories made guerrilla operations difficult, severe Israeli counter-measures and lack of co-operation by the inhabitants of the West Bank prevented them from establishing bases in enemy territory. Although various attempts were made to weld the various resistance groups into a single organisation under al-Fatah's leader Yasir Arafat, no common and agreed military strategy was ever evolved and no single chain of command was established. Two groups in particular—the Popular Front for the Liberation of Palestine led by George Habbash, and the Popular Democratic Front for the Liberation of Palestine—maintained their independence. It was the P.F.L.P. that was responsible for attacks on Israeli civilian aircraft and plane hijackings in 1969 and 1970. The different Palestinian groups were fully united in their rejection of U.N. Security Council Resolution 242 and insisted on their objective of the total liberation of Palestine. In this they were supported by Iraq and Syria. They also came to agree on a common political objective of a non-sectarian, democratic, Palestinian state in which Muslims, Christians and Jews could live together in equality.[10] This would have involved the destruction of the Zionist state, but not the expulsion of the Jews established in Israel who were prepared to accept this objective. Palestinian morale was boosted in March 1968 when the commandos joined forces with the Jordanian army to inflict severe loss on an Israeli retaliatory raiding force at Kerameh in the Jordan valley, but the commando raids on the occupied territories never posed a serious military threat to Israel. Israeli casualties were considerably higher on the Suez Canal front.

The growth of the commando organisations posed a severe internal threat to the régimes in Jordan and Lebanon, where they formed a type of 'state within a state'. A compromise agreement arranged in Cairo in November 1969 between the guerrillas and the Lebanese army was successful in preventing the situation from deteriorating into civil war, although Lebanon continued to suffer from Israeli retaliation raids against guerrilla activity from the south of

the country. In Jordan, on the other hand, a series of agreements between the Palestinian liberation forces and the
Jordanian Government broke down almost as soon as they
were made. In September 1970 a civil war broke out which
was largely provoked by extremists among the Jordanian
army and the guerrillas. Promised Iraqi support for the
Palestinians did not materialise and the Syrian army intervened briefly and ineffectively. Fighting ended with a truce
agreement in Cairo sponsored by Arab heads of state which
apparently left neither side the victor. (President Nasser
died on 28 September immediately after the conclusion of
the agreement.) But over the following months the Jordanian government and army gradually asserted their
authority over the country and restricted the commandos'
base areas. By July 1970 the Palestinian resistance had been
virtually liquidated as a guerrilla force in Jordan. In Syria
and Egypt it was under the control of the regular army and
it was only in South Lebanon that it retained some power
of independent activity.

The decline of the Palestinian liberation movement as a
military force did not mean that the spirit of Palestinian
Arab nationalism had died. Although the 700,000 Palestinians on the West Bank were resigned to Israeli rule they did
not accept it, and the 300,000 in Gaza continued to show
their rejection of it by violent means. Including the Arab
minority in Israel there were now about 1,500,000 Palestinians under Israeli rule, and since the birth rate of the
Palestinian Arabs is much higher than that of the Jews, their
very existence affects the future development of the Zionist
state. Any Arab–Israeli settlement which ignores the separate identity of the Palestinians is unrealistic.

Apart from the revival of Palestinian nationalism the
June 1967 war tended to intensify the radical anti-western
trend in the Arab world. The conservative pro-western
elements among the Arabs did not benefit from the humiliating defeat of Nasser's Egypt because the West—and

especially the United States—was regarded as the principal ally and supporter of Israel. Many Arabs went further to regard Israel as the Trojan horse of western imperialism and the instrument through which it aimed to perpetuate its domination of the Middle East.

On the third day of the Six-Day War King Hussein and President Nasser had agreed on the telephone that there was direct Anglo-American intervention on Israel's side. The U.A.R. broke relations with the U.S.A., and Anglo-American interests came under attack throughout the Arab world. Both Nasser and Hussein later admitted they had been mistaken. (The basis of the charge was that the Jordanians had detected enemy planes on their radar screens in far greater numbers than they thought could be accounted for by the size of the Israeli air force.) But, although Britain's neutrality came to be admitted by most Arab governments (especially after its sponsorship of U.N. Security-Council Resolution 242), hostility towards the U.S. remained undiminished because of the Johnson administration's continued diplomatic, financial and military support for Israel. France's stock rose in the Arab world as a result of its demand for an Israeli withdrawal and its imposition of an arms boycott on Israel for which it had formerly been the major supplier. But it was U.S. policy which was decisive in conditioning the Arab view of the west, and for this reason the Arab–Soviet alliance was strengthened. Although many Arabs were disappointed that the Soviet Union had failed to help them more effectively in June 1967 and the Palestinians in particular were suspicious of its support for a political settlement through Resolution 242, the Egyptian, Syrian and Iraqi governments saw no alternative to seeking Soviet help to redress the balance of Israel's overwhelming military superiority. The deepening Soviet involvement in the Arab world was an inevitable cause of Soviet–Arab friction as the U.S.S.R. seemed in some respects to be taking over the former tutorial role of the western powers. But there seemed little likelihood of the Soviet involvement being reduced in the absence of a general Arab-Israeli settlement.

In the aftermath of the 1967 war the Arab conservatives were on the defensive everywhere. To some extent they were protected from direct criticism of their régimes by the financial aid they were providing to Egypt and the Palestinian organisations, but they had to contend with the radical anti-western trend among their own people.

In Yemen the withdrawal of Egyptian troops did not have the expected result. The Yemeni republicans rallied to beat back the Saudi-supported royalists. The royalists became divided and weakened, and eight years of civil war ended in 1970 with a compromise in favour of the moderate republicans. Saudi Arabia had finally accepted a republic in the Arabian peninsula. As Britain withdrew from South Arabia and finally Aden, one sheikhdom and sultanate after another in the East and West Aden Protectorate fell to the radical republican National Liberation Front. On 30 November 1967 the People's Republic of Southern Yemen came into existence. It moved further leftwards and three years later changed its name to the People's Democratic Republic of Yemen. It was not recognised by Saudi Arabia, and its relations with the more moderate Yemeni Republic deteriorated.

In January 1968 Britain's Labour government announced that it would be withdrawing all its remaining forces from the Persian Gulf by the end of 1971. The withdrawal was confirmed by the Conservatives when they came to power in 1970. The imminent removal of British protection caused the rulers of the small Arab Gulf sheikhdoms to discuss the formation of a federation in self-defence. Because of their failure to devise a federal constitution which would resolve their internal rivalries, Qatar and Bahrain declared their full independence in 1971 and the remaining sheikhdoms of the Trucial Coast formed a Union of Arab Emirates. In

July 1970 the reactionary and isolationist Sultan of Oman
was overthrown by his own son, who declared Oman a fully
independent state. Oman then joined the United Nations.

Two of the few remaining pro-western Arab governments
were eliminated in 1969. In Sudan in May the parliamentary régime was overthrown in a coup led by radical
socialist army officers. The new régime suppressed the
conservative Umma party and moved the country leftwards
towards closer relations with Egypt and the Soviet Union.
An unsuccessful pro-communist coup in July 1971 led to
the suppression of the Sudanese Communist party and
a serious breach with the Soviet Union, but Sudan
remained in the Arab radical camp. In September 1969
the Libyan monarchy was overthrown in a similar coup
of young Nasserist officers led by Colonel Muammar
Qadafy. The new régime reached agreement with Britain
and the U.S.A. for the withdrawal of the last remaining
western military bases on Arab territory. Although a
socialist and radical Arab nationalist Colonel Qadafy was
a deeply religious Muslim, a traditionalist in social matters
and strongly anti-communist. He had much in common
with the Muslim Brothers of the previous generation.

When President Nasser died in September 1970 he was
still the most considerable Arab political figure and his dis-
appearance altered the balance of forces in the Arab world.
For all the diplomatic and military failures of his later years,
which cost some of Egypt's hard-won independence by
placing it so heavily in debt to the Soviet Union, Nasser's
influence on the Middle East and much of the Third World
was profound. To some extent he succeeded in casting Egypt
for the role he had foreseen for it in his *Philosophy of the
Revolution*. But in retrospect his importance may be seen
to lie less in his demonstration that a small power can,
through daring and determined leadership, play a dis-
proportionate role in world affairs, than in the body of
pragmatic social and economic policies which became

known as Arab Socialism. The dismantling of the powers of the old bourgeois and feudal classes, land reform, big strides in industrialisation, the building of the High Dam and above all the instillation into the Egyptians of the feeling that development could be a national enterprise, were the real legacies of the Nasserist Revolution. Certainly there was no part of the Arab world that was too remote to be uninfluenced by them.

Before Nasser's death he had clearly designated Anwar Sadat, one of his former Free Officer colleagues, as his successor by making him the only Vice-President. On Nasser's death Sadat became acting President and then President by a near-unanimous vote of parliament and people. Sadat, whose options were strictly limited by Egypt's difficult circumstances, broadly pursued Nasser's domestic and foreign policies although with some differences of emphasis. Following his successful emergence from a power struggle with Vice-President Ali Sabri and some of his own ministers, he promised to reform Egypt's political system, re-establish the rule of law, and restore public liberties in a number of respects. In foreign policy he faced the same dilemma as his predecessor. While attempting unsuccessfully to persuade the United States to help enforce an Israeli withdrawal, he continued to threaten war as a last resort. Few doubted that he fervently hoped to avoid a battle which could be as disastrous for the Arabs as the last, but he had to consider the impatience of his own people—especially the army and the students.

In November 1970 Syria acquired a more moderate and less isolationist régime when the military wing of the Baath Party led by General Hafez Assad established its authority over the civilian wing. During 1971 Syria, Libya and Egypt moved towards the formation of a tripartite Federation which was finally endorsed by a massive favourable vote in all the three countries on 1 September. Although the Federation aroused much less enthusiasm in the Arab world than earlier attempts at political unity, it seemed to many to be more realistic in structure and to enjoy better chances of lasting. The three states retained their separate identities and constitutions and a federal superstructure was added. Sudan had been associated with the first moves towards federation, but withheld because of strong opposition from communists in the régime. In March 1972 the agreement to bring to an end the prolonged rebellion of Sudan's pre-dominantly non-Arab and non-Muslim southern provinces by granting them regional autonomy pointed to an indefinite postponement of Sudan's adherence to an Arab federation.

Iraq in the early 1970s was somewhat isolated in the Arab world. The chronic political upheavals which followed the 1958 revolution and the intermittent war with the Kurdish minority in northern Iraq prevented the country from realising its great economic potential. The Baathist régime, which recovered power in July 1968, was narrowly based at home and on equally bad terms with Iran, Egypt and the rival Baathists in Syria, although it gained strength by its agreement with the Kurdish nationalists in March 1970. Iraq remains an Arab state of considerable potential importance; in 1972 it showed signs of intending to direct its influence towards the Persian Gulf area. Its position was strengthened in 1972 by increased backing from the Soviet Union. A Soviet–Iraqi treaty of friendship and co-operation was signed in April and the Soviets undertook the development of the major North Rumaiala oil field in southern Iraq, which the Iraq Petroleum Company still claimed as part of its concession.

Saudi Arabia, with its traditional semi-tribal political structure, seemed to stand alone against the stream of Middle Eastern history. King Feisal's personality and diplomatic skill and the continuing strength of traditional Islam among his people helped to stave off the revolution which had overthrown so many Arab monarchies, while the enormous and increasing oil-wealth of the desert kingdom gave it additional status in the Middle East. King Feisal, who remained resolutely anti-communist, was deeply embarrassed by the United States alliance with Israel—especially as most of his wealth came from American oil companies. He endeavoured to promote Islamic unity. In September 1969, following the accidental burning of the al-Aqsa mosque in Jerusalem, one of Islam's holiest shrines, he was the force behind the holding of an Islamic summit meeting at Rabat in Morocco, as an alternative to an Arab summit. A permanent Islamic secretariat was set up in Jedda and regular conferences of Islamic foreign ministers were held thereafter.

THE MAGHRIB

After their achievement of independence the three North African Arab states—Tunisia, Morocco and Algeria—joined the Arab League, but they did not become deeply involved in the affairs of the rest of the Arab world. Their economic ties were still with France and their geographical remoteness prevented them from playing an active role against Israel, however strongly their sympathies lay with the Arab cause.

Tunisia was the least inclined towards Arab nationalism of the three. This was partly due to the personality of President Bourguiba, who was a constant critic of Arab policies (especially Nasserist), and proposed his own brand of moderate pro-westernism (or *Bourguibism*) as an alternative. In 1958 Tunisia joined the Arab League, but immediately withdrew its delegation in protest against Egyptian attitudes. An Egyptian–Tunisian propaganda war continued until 1961 when Nasser's support for Tunisia in the Bizerta incident with France brought about a rapprochement. Despite the clash of personalities between Bourguiba and Nasser there was much in common in their social and economic policies. The new harmony did not last; in April 1965 Bourguiba's suggestion that the Arabs should make peace with Israel as a start towards a solution of the Palestine problem brought angry reactions in many quarters of the Arab world. Hostility towards him was exacerbated by his openly pro-western attitudes, and the feeling that since Tunisia was not directly involved in the Arab–Israeli conflict it could not claim the right to lecture the Arabs on their attitude towards the Palestine question.

Following the Bizerta affair of 1961 and the nationalisation of French property in Tunisia in 1964, France placed Tunisia in a political and economic quarantine. But Franco-Tunisian relations gradually improved; in the early 1970s Tunisia was a moderate single party state aligned economically and politically to the United States and France and heavily dependent on western Europe for markets, tourism and exports of migrant labour. The country took a sharp turn to the right in 1970 with the dismissal and disgrace of Ahmad Ben Salah, the minister responsible for the country's socialist economic policies. Bourguiba, aged sixty-eight in 1972, was in poor health and spent long periods outside the country for medical treatment. But his authority was not seriously challenged, despite widespread student unrest, and the chief political question lay in his choice of successor.

Muhammad V had the important advantage of having been the leader and hero of the Moroccan national movement when he became king of independent Morocco in 1956. The country had no experience of self-government for there had been little constitutional development under the French, and there was an acute lack of trained administrators or professional men. Although in many respects a feudal monarch, Muhammad V succeeded in securing the co-operation for a time of the Moroccan trade unions and left wing politicians. His radical and neutralist foreign policy secured him the friendship of President Nasser, and in 1960 Morocco, the U.A.R., Mali, Guinea and Ghana combined to form the Casablanca group of radical African states. His son Hassan, who succeeded him on his premature death on 21 February 1961, lacked his father's prestige. He took strong constitutional powers into his hands and established an authoritarian form of rule with the support of loyalists and the army but in the face of opposition from the Istiqlal and left wing politicians. The U.A.R.'s sympathies now lay with the independent and socialist republic of Algeria, and, when a frontier dispute led to fighting between Algeria and Morocco in 1963, the U.A.R. supported Algeria. Algerian-Moroccan relations slowly recovered although Morocco's anti-socialist and pro-western policies remained essentially different from those of Algeria.

Morocco's geographical remoteness and the strong monarchic tradition of its people was not sufficient to insulate the country entirely from the radical republican currents in the Arab world. The near success of a military palace coup in June 1971 led to the King's admission of widespread corruption and deficiencies in his régime and the promise of radical social and economic reforms. In the spring of 1972 Hassan II undertook to broaden the base of régime by liberalising the constitution, divesting himself of some of his powers and securing the co-operation of the opposition parties. A further attempt at his violent overthrow, led this time by his right-hand man General Oufkir, underlined the insecurity of his position.

The Algerian Republic which came into being in 1962 enjoyed the high prestige of its heroic struggle for independence but few other advantages. Its colonial economy was even more dependent on France than those of Morocco and Tunisia and it had even fewer trained men and technicians. In 1963 French properties left vacant since 1962, including farms, were taken over by workers' management committees, together with some large agricultural estates still under French management.

In addition to his socialist measures at home Ben Bella pursued a dynamic left wing foreign policy, championing the cause of all anti-colonial liberation movements in Africa. In June 1965 he was overthrown in a bloodless coup led by his own defence minister Houari Boumedienne, a less charismatic and more retiring personality who pursued more cautious policies. He slowed down nationalisation measures and gradually improved relations with France. In 1970 he reached a settlement of the border dispute with Morocco. Algeria obtained most of its military supplies and some economic assistance from the Soviet Union, but its own increasing oil revenues and lack of direct involvement with Israel made it much less dependent than Egypt on the Soviets.

As Algeria under Boumedienne concentrated on tackling its domestic problems and the crash programme for training technicians began to produce results, it became apparent that Algerian natural and human resources provided the potential for rapid economic development and the opportunity to rival Egypt as the first industrial power among the Arab states. By the early 1970s Algeria had gone a long way towards dismantling its colonial-style economic relationship with France. A prolonged dispute with French oil companies in 1971 left Algeria in full control of its own oil industry. But the deep-rooted cultural ties, the widespread use of the French language, and the employment of tens of thousands of Algerians in metropolitan France ensured that a special relationship with France would continue for some time.

11 The Western Muslim World Today

THE peoples of western Islam*—Arabs, Turks and Iranians —are all imbued with a profound sense of their glorious past. They are all inheritors of great empires which in earlier centuries were both more civilised and more powerful than Christian Europe. Following a long period of humiliating Christian ascendancy these peoples have been seeking to bring their present up to the level of their past. The search for dignity has been the essence of these peoples' history in the twentieth century.

The Turks, who declined in power in relation to the West most recently and retained their national self-confidence as a ruling race until the first decades of this century, have been the least affected by this problem. It was the genius of Atatürk to see that if Turkey was to match the overbearing political, economic, and military power of the West, it must first abandon its pretensions to empire and concentrate on its internal development. His secular reforms could not transform all aspects of Turkish society in a single generation (he died in 1938), but in the aftermath of the Second World War it was apparent that in many respects Turkey had become part of Europe. In 1950 parliamentary elections resulted in a sweeping victory for the opposition Democratic Party, which was based on the middle class, private commerce and industry, but had increasing support from the peasantry, over Atatürk's Republican People's Party which had held power for twenty-five years. The Democrats were

* Sometimes referred to as 'Inner Islam' as distinct from the 'Outer Islam' of central and eastern Asia.

fairly popular for the first years of their decade in power. Some state industry set up under Atatürk was denationalised, some concessions were made to religious feeling, and a huge expansion of imports and agricultural credits began. But in 1954 the record run of good harvests ended and inflation started. The urban middle class and the army became increasingly discontented, although the Democratic Party and its leader Adnan Menderes retained the support of the peasantry. Menderes became increasingly dictatorial, and in May 1960 he was ousted by the army. He was tried and hanged the following year.

The military directory did not remain in power. In 1961 it summoned a Constituent Assembly to draft a new constitution, and Turkey retained its parliamentary system, although the army remained watchful in the background. The Justice Party, political heirs of the dissolved Democrat Party, entered a coalition under Atatürk's former right-hand man Ismet İnönü, and in 1965 it came to power on its own under Suleyman Demirel. But Turkish democracy was in peril as it came under increasing fire from left and right. In 1970 Demirel resigned under army pressure, martial law was imposed in several provinces and a repressive campaign was launched against the left. Public liberties were severely restricted, and the very survival of parliamentary democracy hung in the balance. The sharp turn to the right made it seem even less likely that essential social and economic reforms, such as the redistribution of land holdings, which had been repeatedly promised, would be carried out.

Despite the secularisation of the state in Turkey, Islamic feeling remains strong, especially in the countryside. The Democrats and their successors, the Justice Party, reversed some of the secularising measures although they left the fundamental laws unchanged. Even many of the secular intelligentsia would still regard themselves as Muslims; they believe that Turkey has led the way towards an Islamic reformation.[1] However, it must be said that this claim is rejected by many other Muslims (especially Arabs), who hold that Kemalism renounced rather than reformed Islam.

The Iranians were less fortunate than the Turks in that their decline in power took place so much earlier that they were subjected to a long period of alien, predominantly Anglo-Russian, domination. Riza Shah was a man of lesser ability than Atatürk and he was unable to preserve his country's independence and neutrality in the Second World War. Yet the Iranian Empire, for all its variety of races and tongues, has a degree of unity which may be compared with that of Turkey. With the fair level of political stability it has enjoyed for the past two decades and its considerable natural resources (including oil), it has achieved one of the highest rates of economic development among the countries of the Third World. This has helped Iran to assert its independence of Great Power influence. For some years following the overthrow of Mossadegh the Shah was heavily dependent upon the United States for defence against Soviet hostility, but in the late 1960s he reached a rapprochement with the Soviet Union, and in 1967 made an agreement to buy Soviet arms and secured important Soviet aid for Iran's industrialisation, with payment in natural gas. Internally the Shah's rule was centralised and authoritarian; the left wing was severely repressed. But the Shah used his power to achieve what was called his 'White Revolution', notably through agrarian reform and the break-up of the great feudal estates.

It was entirely to be expected that the theme of the celebrations of the 2500th anniversary of the Persian Empire in 1971 should be one of renaissance since Iran had ceased after several centuries to be the helpless puppet of international power politics. While there was no lack of opposition to the Shah's rule and no guarantee of its survival, it seemed likely that Iran's new self-assertiveness would survive even under a different type of régime.

The renaissance of Arab nationalism in the twentieth century has faced far greater obstacles than have Iranian or Turkish nationalism. In contrast to the Iranians and Turks, the Arabs had become accustomed to living under foreign rule following the dissolution of their own empire. In the western Arab world of North Africa the Ottoman imperial masters had already been replaced by western Christian powers in the nineteenth century, and, when the eastern Arabs rose to demand their independence during the First World War, they also found themselves under a western hegemony which in their eyes differed very little from direct colonial rule. Some ninety million Arabs are spread over a vast area from Morocco on the Atlantic to Oman on the Indian Ocean. Much of their land is desert and communications are peculiarly difficult. Many of the new frontiers between the fledgeling states of the twentieth-century Arab world were arbitrarily drawn to suit the interests of the Powers. As one by one these states achieved their political independence, which in most cases was still qualified by the continuation of their economic and military subordination to the West, they were faced with the supremely difficult task of governing themselves without experience, and despite a profound feeling among their peoples that the divisions between them were artificial and ought to be removed. The urge towards Arab unity was deeply emotional, based on a common language, religion,* culture and historical experience, but it faced the most severe practical obstacles to its application. Apart from the difficulties of physical communication, centuries of foreign rule had brought about a diversity of interests and attitudes in different parts of the Arab world. After independence new local interests tended to gather round the governments of

---

* The Muslim religion is a vital element because of the close relation between Arabism and Islam; but Christian Arabs, who are some of the leading spokesmen of Arab nationalism, naturally place less emphasis on this aspect.

even the most artificially created states. Some Arab states, such as Sudan and Iraq, had large non-Arab minorities, which made their inclusion in an Arab union much more difficult.

In 1948 all these barriers to Arab unity were raised infinitely higher by the creation of the Zionist state of Israel. Superficially Israel might seem to unite the Arabs in a common enmity, but in much more important respects it keeps them apart. It not only forms an impenetrable physical barrier between the Arabs of Asia and Africa, but, in diverting so much of their physical and emotional energies into the cause of restoring Arab Palestine, has prevented them from seeking practical means of overcoming the obstacles to Arab unity.

This suggests some of the reasons for the apparently chronic political instability of many Arab states. This has not prevented social and economic development. The restructuring of Arab society may not have been as profound as many Arab progressive and liberal intellectuals would wish, but there can be no doubt that it has been taking place. Two factors have been especially powerful in promoting change. One has been the spread of modern secular education at all levels in even the most conservatively inclined of the Arab states. Arab governments of various political colours have devoted a high proportion of their budgets to education in response to a strong popular demand. The increase in girls' education in the Muslim Arab states has been especially revolutionary. In the early 1970s the result could be seen in the existence of a rapidly expanding and increasingly influential Arab professional middle class.[2] In almost every Arab state these new-style 'technocrats' were replacing those of the traditional bourgeois politicians who remained in the government.

The other element of change was the oil industry. A decision of the Creator has placed some sixty per cent of the world's crude oil reserves under the soil of the Muslim states of the Middle East and North Africa—including some of those most sparsely populated and lacking in other natural resources. Some of the vast wealth this produced was misused in the early stages on ostentatious display, but today it is mostly diverted into social and economic development and is accelerating the pace of transformation of Arab society. It has also placed considerable economic and political power in the hands of the oil-producing states, which have learned to exercise this power with increasing effectiveness through O.P.E.C. (the Organisation of the Petroleum Exporting Countries), which was created in 1960. The emergence of a corps of experienced native oil technocrats has also enabled these countries to take over the management of their oil industries from the western concessionaire companies, which for so long were symbols of western political and economic domination.

The immense increase in oil revenues has made it possible for some of the Arab states with small populations, such as Kuwait, Qatar, and Abu Dhabi, to transform themselves socially and economically in less than a generation, despite their lack of resources other than oil. Through the oil industry Saudi Arabia has achieved power and political influence out of all proportion to its natural capabilities. Much of the oil wealth has spread and is spreading to other parts of the Arab world through private investment, public investment (through institutions such as the Kuwait Arab Development Fund) or direct government subsidies, such as those paid to Egypt by Kuwait, Saudi Arabia and Libya since 1967. All the present indications are that the growth in oil revenues, with all its social side-effects, will continue for at least another generation.

Economic nationalism in the Arab world, like political nationalism, has in the past usually meant reducing dependence on the West. The process was seen first most clearly in Egypt in 1956 with the take-over of the still considerable French and British interests, followed shortly afterwards by

the 'Egyptianisation' of almost the whole economy. Syria
and Iraq have followed Egypt's example. In each case the
trend has resulted in closer economic ties with the Soviet
Union and the East European states. Since the Soviet Union
undertook to help build the High Dam in 1958 (following
the withdrawal of the offer of western aid), it has expanded
its relations with nearly all the Arab states as a trading
partner, and for some it has become the major source of
financial and technical aid for their economic development
programmes. Only the major oil producers, such as Saudi
Arabia, Kuwait and Libya, are able to dispense with aid
from West or East.

In every Arab state which adopted or inherited a form of
western parliamentary democracy this has been abandoned.*
In many of them (Egypt, Syria, Iraq, Libya, Sudan, Yemen)
the established régime—whether monarchy or republic—
has been overthrown by the army, but, although the officers
or ex-officers may continue to play an important role in
government, none has a purely military régime. Army rule
has received no more enthusiastic support in the Arab world
than did the discarded type of parliamentary democracy.
Tribalism has declined in all areas, although it survives with
some strength in parts of Arabia.

Arab governments, whether conservative monarchist or
socialist republican, tend towards authoritarianism, and
public liberties are restricted to varying degrees in every
Arab state. It may be said that each of them is searching
for a viable political system and has yet to find it. Most of
them are doing so under the severe handicap of having
become nations so recently. The emotional urge towards
Arab unity (much stronger in the eastern than in the western

* With the qualified exception of Lebanon where it is the only
form of constitution which would ensure the representation in
government and legislature of the country's various sects. The experience of Turkey, where the West European style of parliamentary
democracy which was adopted in the 1950s and is now under exceptional stress, is being observed with interest in the Arab countries.

half of the Arab world) is also a factor of instability because the sense of patriotism and civic responsibility of most Arabs is diluted by the feeling that the state to which they belong must one day be merged into a larger unit. In realistic terms this may be a remote ideal, but it exerts a powerful psychological influence.

The impulse for Arab political unity has been reflected in the economic field, but is hampered by the lack of complimentarity between the economies of the Arab states. An Economic Unity Agreement was signed in 1962 by Jordan, Egypt, Morocco, Kuwait and Syria and later adhered to by Yemen, Iraq and Sudan. The aims were similar to those of the E.E.C.—the abolition of internal tariffs and the complete freedom of movement of labour and capital. Another agreement establishing an Arab Common Market was signed in 1965 by Egypt, Jordan, Iraq, Kuwait, and Syria. Yemen and Sudan have since adhered to the agreement, but the Kuwaiti National Assembly voted against ratification. Considerable progress has been made towards reducing tariffs between members, but freedom of movement of labour remains a more distant goal.

In some important, but unglamorous and unpublicised, respects the Arab states are strengthening the links between them. The new generation of Arab experts or technocrats, who come together at the annual Arab Petroleum Congress, engineers' and lawyers' conferences or similar meetings, are the contemporary equivalent of the Ottoman élite. Attempts to improve inter-Arab communications of all kinds are making real, if uneven, progress. Almost certainly closer Arab unity will be achieved through a gradual strengthening of the links between peoples and institutions rather than through the dramatic mergers of governments.

There has been some trend towards secularisation of the educational and legal systems in all states, including those such as Saudi Arabia where the hold of orthodox religion is strongest. The Islamic Sharia, for example, cannot fulfil all the needs of a modern socialist or capitalist economy. But no Arab state—Nasser's Egypt, Baathist Iraq or Syria, Bourguiba's Tunisia or even the semi-marxist régime in South Yemen—has proceeded so far with secularisation as Kemalist Turkey. In every case, with the exception of half-Christian Lebanon, Islam remains the official religion of the state. While there was an important secular element in Nasser's political outlook, he was a gradualist who respected the strength of traditional opinion. He was also, in contrast to Atatürk, a Muslim believer. Both he and some other Arab national leaders, such as Bourguiba, would have liked to quicken the pace of secularisation especially in such matters as the personal status of women, divorce and polygamy, but have refrained in order to avoid the possibility of an Islamic backlash. As we have seen, the youngest revolutionary régime in the Arab world in Libya has turned its back on secularism to place a renewed emphasis on Islam. The strength of the Islamic element in the Algerian Revolution was widely underestimated. Because Algerian women played an important role in the struggle, their emancipation in independent Algeria was expected to advance more rapidly than has happened. In all the Arab countries which were under French rule the emphasis since independence has been on the Arabisation of education to undo the effects of the imposition of French culture on a Muslim Arab society.

Arab socialism, as it has been, and is being, developed by Nasserists, Baathists and the other 'progressive' Arab régimes, is no rigid doctrine, but an attempt to reconcile contemporary ideals of social justice and equality with Arab traditions and Islamic principles. It seeks to adopt some elements of marxism while rejecting its fundamental view of the perfectibility of a classless society on earth. For these reasons Arab marxists tend to take a scornful view of the achievements of Arab progressive régimes, which they regard as dictatorships of the new bourgeoisie. For good or ill this new middle class of army officers, technocrats and civil servants, which has largely displaced the traditional Middle Eastern élite of kings, landowners and bourgeoisie, seems likely to consolidate the hold it has gained on political power. It is always possible that the Maoist type of revolutionary mass peasant movement, which is advocated by marxists as the only realistic solution to the social and economic problems of the Arab states, may arise, but hitherto there has been very little sign of this happening in any predominantly Muslim society.

Chronological Table

1830		French conquest of Algeria.
1833		Treaty of Hunkiar Iskelessi.
1839		Britain occupies Aden.
1860		French landings in Lebanon.
1869		Opening of Suez Canal.
1876		Abdul Hamid II succeeds to the throne.
1878		Cyprus Convention.
1881		French occupation of Tunisia.
1882		British occupation of Egypt.
1898		Reconquest of Sudan.
		Anglo-Egyptian Condominium.
1907		Anglo-Russian agreement on Persia.
		Lord Cromer retires from Egypt.
1908		Hejaz Railway completed.
		Young Turks Revolt.
1909		Abdul Hamid deposed.
1911		Al-Fatat founded in Paris.
1912		France declares Moroccan Protectorate.
		Italian occupation of Libya.
		Commercial oil production begins in Persia.
1913		Ibn Saud occupies al-Hasa.
1914	October	Turkey declares war on Allies.
	December	British Protectorate over Egypt.
1915		Dardanelles campaign.
1915–16		Hussein–McMahon correspondence.
1916	May	Sykes–Picot agreement.
	June	Arab revolt begins.
1917	January	Allies recognise Hussein as King of Hejaz.
	March	Baghdad falls to Allies.

1917	November	Balfour Declaration.
	December	Jerusalem taken.
1918	January	President Wilson's Fourteen Points.
	October	Damascus, Beirut and Aleppo taken.
		Treaty of Mudros.
	November	Anglo-French Declaration.
1919		Versailles Peace Conference.
	January	Emir Feisal asks for Arab independence.
	March–	
	April	Egyptian uprising.
	May	Greeks land at Izmir.
1920	March	General Syrian Congress declares Syrian independence under Feisal.
	April	San Remo Conference. Mandates for Syria, Lebanon, Iraq and Palestine declared.
	May–	
	August	Iraqi uprising. First riots in Palestine.
	July	French occupy Damascus.
	August	'Le Grand Liban' declared.
		Treaty of Sèvres.
1920–2		Greco-Turkish war.
1921	February	Soviet–Persian Treaty. Riza Shah seizes power.
	March	Cairo Conference.
		Abdullah recognised as Emir of Transjordan.
	August	Feisal becomes King of Iraq.
1922	February	Britain recognises qualified Egyptian independence.
	October	Anglo-Iraqi Treaty.
		Final Turkish defeat of Greeks.
	November	Ottoman Sultanate abolished.
1923	May	Transjordan independent under British protection.
	July	Treaty of Lausanne.
	October	Turkey declared Republic.
1924	March	Caliphate abolished.
	October	Ibn Saud seizes Hejaz from Hussein.
1925	July	Syrian revolt against French.

1926	January	Ibn Saud declared King of Hejaz.
	May	Lebanese Republic declared.
	July	Anglo-Iraqi-Turkish Treaty.
	October	Riza Shah replaces Qajar shahs of Persia.
1927	May	Anglo-Saudi Treaty.
	April	Zaghlul dies.
1928		Turkey becomes secular state.
1929		Arab-Jewish violence in Palestine.
1930	May	France declares Syrian constitution.
	June	Anglo-Iraqi Treaty.
1932		Iraq becomes independent.
1934		Saudi–Yemeni war.
		Anglo-Yemeni treaty.
1936–9		Arab revolt in Palestine.
1936	August	Anglo-Egyptian Treaty.
	September	Franco-Syrian Treaty (never ratified).
	November	Franco-Lebanese Treaty (never ratified).
	October	Bakr Sidqi revolt in Iraq.
1937		First major oil discovery in Saudi Arabia.
		Peel Report recommends partition of Palestine.
1938		Oil discovered in Kuwait.
1939	May	British White Paper on Palestine.
	June	Alexandretta (Iskanderun) incorporated into Turkey.
1941	April	Golden Square revolt in Iraq.
	June–July	Allied forces occupy Lebanon and Syria.
	August	Anglo-Russian forces enter Iran.
	September	Riza Shah abdicates.
1942	January	Anglo-Russian-Iranian treaty of alliance.
	February	King Farouk forced to instal Wafd Government.
	November	Anglo-American invasion of North Africa.
1943		Lebanese National Pact.

1943	February	Algerian nationalists present claims.
	December	Moroccan Istiqlal Party created.
		Arab Baath Party founded.
1944	November	Moroccan nationalists demand independence.
1944–6		France hands over power to independent Syria and Lebanon.
1945	March	Arab League formed.
	May	Setif massacre in Algeria.
		Anglo-American forces withdraw from Iran.
1946		Transjordan declared independent.
		Last Soviet forces leave Iran.
1947	March	Truman doctrine promulgated.
	September	Algerian statute.
	October	Truman doctrine extended to Iran.
	November	U.N. General Assembly Palestine partition resolution.
1948	May	British Palestine mandate ends. Israel created.
1949	March–July	Israel concludes armistice agreements with Egypt, Syria, Transjordan and Lebanon.
	March	Military coup in Syria.
1950	April	Hashemite Kingdom of Jordan created.
	December	Fifty-fifty profit-sharing introduced in Saudi oil industry.
1951	April	Iranian oil nationalised.
	July	King Abdullah assassinated.
	October	Egypt repudiates 1936 treaty.
	December	Libya declared independent kingdom.
1952	January	Burning of Cairo.
	July	Free officers overthrow Egyptian monarchy. Egyptian land reform.
1953	February	Anglo-Egyptian agreement on Sudan.
	August	Mossadegh falls.
	November	Ibn Saud dies.
1954	July	Tunisian autonomy.
		Anglo-Egyptian agreement on Suez.

1954	November	Algerian revolt begins.
1954–62		Algerian War.
1955	February–November	Baghdad Pact formed.
	February	Israel's Gaza raid.
	April	Nasser attends Bandung Conference.
	September	Egypt's Czech arms deal.
1956	January	Sudan becomes independent republic.
	March	Last British troops leave Egypt.
		Morocco and Tunisia declared independent.
	July	Nationalisation of Suez Canal.
	October–November	Franco-British-Israel invasion of Egypt.
	October	Anglo-Jordanian Treaty terminated.
1957	January	Eisenhower doctrine promulgated.
	July	Tunisian Republic proclaimed.
1958	February	Syria and Egypt form United Arab Republic.
	March	King Saud relinquishes powers to Prince Feisal.
	May–October	Lebanese crisis.
	July	Iraqi Revolution. Republic declared.
		American landings in Lebanon.
		British landings in Jordan.
1961	July	Bizerta affair.
	September	Syria secedes from U.A.R.
1962	May	Egypt's National Charter.
	July	Algeria becomes independent.
	September	Yemeni coup. Republican-royalist civil war begins.
1963	January	Aden merged with South Arabian Federation.
	February	Kassem overthrown by Baathist-led coalition.
	March	Syrian Baathists return to power.
	March–April	Syrian–Iraqi–U.A.R. union talks.

	November	Iraqi Baathists ousted.
1964	January	First Arab Summit meeting.
	July	African Summit in Cairo.
	October	Non-aligned Summit in Cairo.
	September	Second Arab Summit. United Arab Military Command and Palestine Liberation Organisation created.
1965	January	Al-Fatah's first military communiqué.
	June	Ben Bella overthrown by Colonel Boumedienne.
1966	February	Radical Baathist coup in Syria.
	Autumn	Violence in Aden.
1967	June	Arab–Israeli War. Suez Canal closed.
	August	Arab Summit meeting in Khartoum.
	November	Egyptians withdraw from Yemen.
		British withdraw from Aden.
		People's Republic of South Yemen declared.
		U.N. Security Council Resolution 242 adopted.
1968	January	Britain announces withdrawal from Persian Gulf by 1971.
	March	Battle of Kerameh.
	July	Iraq Baathists return to power.
1969	May	Radical nationalist coup in Sudan.
	September	Islamic Summit meeting in Rabat.
		Libyan monarchy overthrown.
	December	Arab Summit meeting breaks down.
1970	March	Iraq-Kurdish agreement.
	May	Yemeni civil war ends in compromise.
	August	Egyptian–Jordanian–Israeli ceasefire.
	September	President Nasser dies.
		Jordanian-Palestinian civil war.
1971	July	Palestinian guerrilla bases in Jordan liquidated.
		Attempted army coup in Morocco.
	September	Syrian–Libyan–Egyptian Federation formed.
1972	July	Egypt expels Soviet advisers.

References

1 THE BACKGROUND

1. J. Carmichael, *The Shaping of the Arabs* (London 1967), pp. 1-2.
2. Sir Thomas W. Arnold, *The Caliphate 632-1924* (London 1965), p. 164.
3. B. Lewis, *The Emergence of Modern Turkey* (London 1968), pp. 22-3.
4. Ibid. p. 28.
5. J. C. Hurewitz, *Diplomacy in the Near and Middle East* (London 1956), vol. i, p. 106.
6. Ibid. pp. 112-13.
7. Ibid. pp. 164-5.
8. Ibid. pp. 187-8.
9. Ibid. pp. 64-5.
10. A. Hourani, *Arabic Thought in the Liberal Age 1798-1939* (London 1962), pp. 25-33.

2 THE OTTOMAN EMPIRE 1900-1914

1. G. Antonius, *The Arab Awakening: The Story of the Arab National Movement* (Beirut 1962), p. 65.
2. Hurewitz, i, p. 265-7.
3. P. Mansfield, *The British in Egypt* (London 1971), pp. 164-5.
4. D. de Rivoyre, *Les Vrais Arabes et leur Pays*, pp. 294-5, quoted in Antonius, p. 90.
5. Arnold, p. 174.
6. Hourani, ch. 5.
7. Antonius, p. 72.
8. Lewis, pp. 201-2.
9. Antonius, p. 104.
10. Ibid. p. 101.
11. Sir Ronald Storrs, *Orientations* (London 1937), p. 143.
12. A. L. Tibawi, *Islamic Education* (London 1972), p. 84.
13. Ibid. p. 85.

3   THE END OF EMPIRE 1914–1920

1. Storrs, pp. 149–52.
2. Hurewitz, ii, pp. 17–18.
3. See Antonius, ch. 16, and Ann Williams, *Britain and France in the Middle East and North Africa* (London 1968), p. 13. For full text of correspondence see Antonius, Appendix A.
4. See E. Kedourie, *England and the Middle East: the Destruction of the Ottoman Empire 1914–21* (London 1956), ch. 2.
5. Z. N. Zeine, *The Struggle for Arab Independence* (Beirut 1960), pp. 6–10.
6. Antonius, pp. 186–7.
7. *Documents on British Foreign Policy (D.B.F.P.)*, i, iv, pp. 245–47.
8. Antonius, p. 252.
9. Hurewitz, ii, pp. 36–7.
10. Antonius, p. 241.
11. Hurewitz, ii, p. 29.
12. Ibid. ii, p. 30.
13. Ibid. ii, p. 26.
14. See L. Stein, *The Balfour Declaration* (London 1961), and M. Vereté, *Middle East Studies* vol. 6, no. 1 (January 1970).
15. See Palestine Papers 1917–22: *Seeds of Conflict* (London 1972). Compiled and annotated by D. Ingrams, p. 46.
16. *D.B.F.P.*, i, iv.
17. C. Sykes, *Crossroads to Israel* (London 1965), pp. 38–9.
18. Antonius, pp. 437–9.
19. Hurewitz, ii, pp. 66–74.
20. *D.B.F.P.*, i, iv, 340–2.
21. Hurewitz, ii, pp. 62–4.
22. Quoted by D. Lloyd George, *Memoirs*, ii, pp. 1113–14.
23. Kedourie, pp. 152–5.
24. Sykes, p. 207.
25. Hurewitz, ii, p. 107.
26. Ibid. ii, pp. 111–14.
27. Ibid, ii, pp. 143–6.
28. Mansfield, p. 220.
29. Ibid. p. 222.
30. See Lord Wavell, *Allenby in Egypt* (London 1944), ch. 4.

4   TURKEY RESURGENT

1. Hurewitz, ii, p. 31.
2. Lewis, pp. 236–7.
3. Hurewitz, ii, pp. 81–9.

4. Ibid. ii, pp. 119-27.
5. Arnold, p. 180.
6. See W. C. Smith, *Islam in Modern History* (Princeton 1957), ch. 4.
7. A. Mango, *Turkey* (London 1968), pp. 133-4.

5 THE ARAB STRUGGLE FOR INDEPENDENCE
   1920-1939

1. *The Memoirs of the Aga Khan* (London 1954), pp. 153-4.
2. Nicola Ziadeh, *Syria and Lebanon* (London 1957), p. 51.
3. Ibid. p. 51.
4. Hurewitz, ii, pp. 211-14.
5. Ibid. ii, pp. 226-9.
6. Ibid. ii, pp. 178-81.
7. E. Be'eri, *Army Officers in Arab Politics and Society* (London 1970), pp. 15-20.
8. G. Stocking, *Middle East Oil* (London 1971), ch. 2.
9. Hurewitz, ii, pp. 203-11.
10. For Anglo-Saudi Treaty, see Hurewitz, ii, pp. 148-50.
11. Stocking, ch. 3.
12. Ibid. ch. 4.
13. H. St J. Philby, *Saudi Arabia* (London 1955), pp. 322-4.
14. Hurewitz, ii, pp. 196-7.
15. Ibid. ii, pp. 64-6.
16. Ibid. ii, pp. 90-4.
17. Stocking, ch. 1.
18. Sykes, pp. 108-12.
19. Government of Palestine, *Statistical Abstract of Palestine, 1941* (London), p. 12.
20. Ibid. p. 12.
21. Sykes, p. 156
22. Cmd. 5479 (London 1937).
23. Cmd. 6019 (London 1939).

6 THE SECOND WORLD WAR

1. Ziadeh, p. 65.
2. Ibid. pp. 65-7.
3. Hurewitz, ii, pp. 237-8.
4. Government of Palestine, *A Survey of Palestine* (London 1946), ii, pp. 590-1.
5. Hurewitz, ii, pp. 245-9.
6. Nevill Barbour (ed.), *A Survey of North-West Africa* (London 1959), p. 220.

7 POST-WAR UNSETTLEMENT

1. Hurewitz, ii, pp. 273–5.
2. Stocking, p. 155.
3. Report of Anglo-American Committee of Enquiry, 20 April 1946, U.S. Government Printing Office (Washington 1946).
4. U.N. General Assembly Resolution 181 (iii).
5. Government of Palestine, *Statistical Abstract of Palestine, 1945* (London).
6. Sykes, p. 370.
7. U.N. General Assembly Resolution 194 (iii).
8. P. Seale, *The Struggle for Syria* (London, 1965), p. 45.
9. Hurewitz, ii, pp. 329–32.

8 THE RISE OF NASSERISM

1. P. Mansfield, *Nasser's Egypt* (London 1969), pp. 200–1.
2. Cmd. 8904 (London 1953).
3. Cmd. 9298 (London 1954).
4. See G. Adbul Nasser, *Egypt's Liberation: The Philosophy of the Revolution* (Buffalo 1959).
5. Hurewitz, ii, pp. 390–5.
6. See K. Love, *Suez the Twice-Fought War* (London 1970), pp. 5–20.
7. U.N. General Assembly Resolution 1000 (ES-1).
8. See K. S. Abu Jaber, *The Arab Baath Socialist Party* (New York 1966).
9. M. Kerr, *The Arab Cold War 1958–64* (London 1965), pp. 28–34.
10. Mansfield, *Nasser's Egypt*, ch. 9.
11. Ibid. ch. 11.
12. *The Charter*, English translation (Cairo 1962), p. 36.
13. Ibid. pp. 53–6.
14. Ibid. pp. 43–6.
15. Ibid. p. 73.

9 NORTH AFRICA WINS INDEPENDENCE

1. Barbour, p. 304.
2. Ibid. p. 304.
3. Ibid. p. 161.

4. S. Amin, *The Maghreb in the Modern World* (London 1971), p. 111.
5. Barbour, p. 231.
6. Amin, p. 129.

10 THE ARAB WORLD 1962–1972

1. T. Little, *South Arabia* (London 1968), pp. 42–4.
2. Ibid. p. 59.
3. D. Holden, *Farewell to Arabia* (London 1966), p. 56.
4. See Kerr, ch. 3.
5. Ibid. p. 117.
6. Mansfield, *Nasser's Egypt*, p. 54.
7. M. Rodinson, *Israel and the Arabs* (London 1968), p. 181.
8. See M. Howard and R. Hunter, *Israel and the Arab World: The Crisis of 1967*, Adelphi Papers, October 1967, pp. 27–39. See also E. Rouleau, J.-F. Held and J. and S. Lacouture, *Israel et les Arabes – le 3me Combat* (Paris 1967); and W. Laqueur, *The Road to War 1967* (London 1968). These various accounts of the June 1967 war give different interpretations, but agree in general on its causes.
9. See H. Cattan, *Palestine, the Arabs and Israel*, pp. 107–15.
10. See *Revolutionary Lessons and Trials*, vol. i (published by the Palestine Liberation Front 1968).

11 THE WESTERN MUSLIM WORLD TODAY

1. W. C. Smith, *Islam in Modern History* (Princeton 1957), p. 161.
2. M. Halpern, *The Politics of Social Change in the Middle East and North Africa* (Princeton 1963), pp. 51–79.

Bibliography

1. DOCUMENTS

H. M. DAVIS, *Constitutions, Electoral Laws, Treaties of States in the Near and Middle East* (Cambridge 1947; 2nd edn 1953, Durham, N. Carolina).

Documents diplomatiques français 1871–1914, 2ᵉ serie, *1901–1914* (Ministère des Affaires Etrangères, Paris 1948).

G. P. GOOCH and H. W. V. TEMPERLEY, *British Documents on the Origins of the War 1898–1914*, vols ix and x (London 1936).

J. C. HUREWITZ, *Diplomacy in the Near and Middle East*, vol. i, 1535–1914; vol. ii, 1914–1956 (Princeton 1956). These include all the important agreements affecting the Near and Middle East during these periods.

E. L. WOODWARD and ROHAN BUTLER (eds), *Documents on British Foreign Policy 1919–1939* (London H.M.S.O.).

2. MEMOIRS

ABDULLAH IBN AL-HUSSEIN, *The Memoirs of King Abdullah of Transjordan*, ed. by P. P. Graves (London 1950). *My Memoirs Completed* (al-Takmilah), trans. H. W. Glidden (Washington 1954).

LADY BELL (ed.), *Letters of Gertrude Bell*, 2 vols (London 1927): the prominent teacher and Arabist who played a leading role in Britain's Iraqi mandate.

SIR CHARLES BELGRAVE, *Personal Column* (London 1960): adviser to the Ruler of Bahrain, 1926–57.

N. and H. BENTWICH, *Mandate Memories 1914–48* (London 1965) : Attorney General of Palestine (1922–31) and wife.

Lt.-Gen. E. L. M. BURNS, *Between Arab and Israeli* (London 1962) : Chief of Staff of U.N. Truce Supervision Organisation 1954–6; Commander of U.N. Emergency Force 1956.

GENERAL G. CATROUX, *Deux Missions en Moyen Orient 1919–22* (Paris 1958) : a senior French officer-administrator.

R. H. S. CROSSMAN, *Palestine Mission* (London 1947) : the British Labour politician and writer, who was a member of the Anglo-American Committee of Enquiry on Palestine.

C. V. EDMONDS, *Kurds, Turks and Arabs: Politics, Travel and Research in North Eastern Iraq, 1919–1925* (London 1957).

J. B. GLUBB, *A Soldier with the Arabs* (London 1957) : the former Commander of the Arab Legion.

DAVID BEN GURION, *Rebirth and Destiny of Israel* (first English edn, London 1959) : Israel's first Prime Minister.

KING HUSSEIN OF JORDAN, *Uneasy Lies the Head* (London 1962).

D. INGRAMS, *A Time in Arabia* (London 1970) : especially interesting for descriptions of South Arabian women.

SIR ALEC KIRKBRIDE, *A Crackle of Thorns* (London 1964) : British administrator in Transjordan between the two world wars.

T. E. LAWRENCE, *Seven Pillars of Wisdom* (London 1935) : Lawrence of Arabia's account of the Arab Revolt and his role in it; a literary masterpiece but not always accurate.

J. G. McDONALD, *My Mission in Israel 1948–1951* (New York 1951) : first U.S. Ambassador to Israel.

R. M. MEINERTZHAGEN, *Middle East Diary 1917–1956* (London 1959) : member of British Peace Conference staff after the First World War.

GAMAL ABDUL NASSER, *Egypt's Liberation: The Philosophy of the Revolution* (Buffalo 1959) : Nasser's political ideas and aims at the outset of his career.

MOHAMMED NEGUIB, *Egypt's Destiny* (London 1955) : the Egyptian general who officially led the 1952 Revolution.

Mohammed Riza Pahlevi (Shah of Persia), *Mission for My Country* (London 1960).

H. St J. B. Philby, *Arabian Jubilee* (London 1952); *Forty Years in the Wilderness* (London 1957) : a British traveller and scholar who devoted his life to Arabia.

A. Sadat, *Revolt on the Nile* (London 1957) : Nasser's fellow-revolutionary who succeeded him.

Sir Ronald Storrs, *Orientations* (London 1937) : served in Arabia, Cairo and Palestine in the First World War and after.

K. Trevaskis, *Shades of Amber* (London 1968) : British administrator in South Arabia.

D. Van der Meulen, *Aden to the Hadhramaut* (London 1947) : a Dutch expert on Arabia.

Chaim Weizmann, *Trial and Error* (London 1949) : the creation of Israel recounted by its first President.

Sir Arnold T. Wilson, *Loyalties: Mesopotamia 1914–1917* (London 1930); *Mesopotamia 1917–1920: A Clash of Loyalties* (London 1931) : a controversial British official in Iraq.

A. E. Yalman, *Turkey in my Time* (Norman, Oklahoma 1956) : an eminent Turkish liberal, editor of *Vatan*.

3. GENERAL

G. Antonius, *The Arab Awakening: The Story of the Arab National Movement* (Beirut 1962) : a pro-Hashemite account of the Arab political revival in the twentieth century; very influential.

A. J. Arberry (ed.), *Religion in the Middle East*, 2 vols (Cambridge 1969).

Sir Thomas W. Arnold, *The Caliphate 632–1924* (London 1965).

J. S. Badeau, *The American Approach to the Arab World* (New York 1968) : an American scholar-diplomat.

G. Baer, *Population and Society in the Arab East* (London 1964).

E. Be'eri, *Army Officers in Arab Politics and Society* (London 1970) : a comprehensive account by an Israeli.

M. Berger, *The Arab World Today* (New York 1962) : a useful social study.

J. Berque, *The Arabs: Their History and Future* (London 1964) : an important work by a major French Islamic scholar.

D. C. Blaisdell, *European Financial Control in the Ottoman Empire* (2nd edn, New York 1966).

A. Bonne, *State and Economics in the Middle East* (2nd edn, London 1960).

Cambridge History of Islam, 2 vols (Cambridge 1971).

C. S. Coon, *Caravan: The Story of the Middle East* (rev. edn, New York 1962).

N. J. Coulson, *History of Islamic Law* (Edinburgh 1964).

S. N. Fisher (ed.), *Social Forces in the Middle East* (New York 1968).

W. B. Fisher, *The Middle East: A Physical, Social and Regional Geography* (6th edn, London 1971).

H. A. R. Gibb, *Modern Trends in Islam* (Chicago 1947); *Mohammedanism* (2nd rev. edn, London 1969) : two important works by an outstanding Islamic scholar.

S. D. F. Goitein, *Jews and Arabs: Their Contacts through the Ages* (New Work 1955) : a useful history of Arab–Jewish relations.

S. G. Haim (ed.), *Arab Nationalism, An Anthology* (Berkeley 1962) : a valuable collection of translated texts.

M. Halpern, *The Politics of Social Change in the Middle East and North Africa* (Princeton 1963) : an analysis of the modern development of western Islamic society.

Z. Y. Hershlag, *Contemporary Economic Structure of the Middle East* (Leiden 1971).

P. K. Hitti, *History of the Second World War: The Mediterranean and Middle East*, vol. i (London 1954); *History of the Arabs* (10th edn, London 1970).

H.L. Hoskins, *British Routes to India* (2nd edn, London 1966) : Britain's strategic and economic interest in the Middle East.

A. H. Hourani, *Minorities in the Arab World* (London 1947); *Arabic Thought in the Liberal Age 1798–1939*

(London 1962): the influence of English and French liberal ideas on Arab writers and intellectuals.

E. Kedourie, *England and the Middle East: The Destruction of the Ottoman Empire 1914–1921* (London 1956): a neo-imperial view of the effect of the First World War on the Middle East.

M. H. Kerr, *The Arab Cold War* (London 1969): the Syrian–Egyptian union and its aftermath.

G. E. Kirk, *A Short History of the Middle East* (7th edn, London 1964): to be used with caution. *The Middle East in the War 1939–46* (London 1953). *The Middle East 1945–50* (London 1954).

H. Kohn, *Nationalism and Imperialism in the Hither East* (London 1932).

W. Z. Laqueur, *Communism and Nationalism in the Middle East* (London 1956): the standard work to date. *The Road to War, 1967* (London 1967); *The Struggle for the Middle East: The Soviet Union and the Middle East 1958–68* (London 1969).

G. Lenczowski, *The Middle East in World Affairs* (2nd edn, Ithaca, N.Y. 1956).

R. Levy, *The Social Structure of Islam*, being the 2nd edn of *The Sociology of Islam* (Cambridge 1957).

B. Lewis, *The Arabs in History* (4th edn, London 1968).

S. H. Longrigg, *Oil in the Middle East* (3rd edn, London 1968): a history by a British pioneer oil administrator.

D. B. MacDonald, *Development of Muslim Theology, Jurisprudence and Constitutional Theory* (Lahore 1960).

P. Mansfield (ed.), *The Middle East: A Political and Economic Survey* (London 1973).

A. Mez, *The Renaissance of Islam*, tr. by S. H. Bakhsh and D. S. Margoliouth (London 1937).

E. Monroe, *The Mediterranean in Politics* (London 1938); *Britain's Moment in the Middle East 1914–56* (London 1963): a penetrating analysis.

H. Z. Nuseibeh, *The Ideas of Arab Nationalism* (New York 1956).

W. R. Polk, and R. L. Chambers (eds.), *The United States and the Arab World* (Cambridge, Mass. 1965); *Beginnings of Modernization in the Middle East: The Nineteenth Century* (Chicago 1968).

F. RAHMAN, *Islam* (London 1966) : a useful Muslim viewpoint.

M. RODINSON, *Israel and the Arabs* (London 1968) : a noted French Islamicist's survey.

E. I. J. ROSENTHAL, *Islam in the National State* (Cambridge 1965).

B. SHWADRAN, *The Middle East, Oil and the Great Powers* (2nd rev. edn, New York 1959).

W. C. SMITH, *Islam in Modern History* (Princeton 1957) : original and thought-provoking.

G. W. STOCKING, *Middle East Oil: A Study in Political and Economic Controversy* (London 1971).

A. L. TIBAWI, *Islamic Education* (London 1972) : short but excellent.

A. V. TOYNBEE, *A Study of History*; abridgement of vols i–vi by D. C. Somervell (London 1946).

G. E. VON GRUNEBAUM (ed.), *Unity and Variety in Muslim Civilisation* (Chicago 1956).

D. WARRINER, *Land Reform and Development in the Middle East: A Study of Egypt, Syria and Iraq* (2nd edn, London 1962) : an outstanding study of a key socio-economic question. *Land Reform in Principle and Practice* (Oxford 1968).

A. WILLIAMS, *Britain and France in The Middle East and North Africa* (London 1968).

Z. N. ZEINE, *The Struggle for Arab Independence: Western Diplomacy and the Rise and Fall of Faisal's Kingdom in Syria* (Beirut 1960); *The Emergence of Arab Nationalism* (Beirut 1966) : two useful studies by a Beirut historian.

4. STUDIES ON INDIVIDUAL COUNTRIES
(listed alphabetically)

Arabia

B. C. BUSCH, *Britain and the Persian Gulf 1894–1914* (Berkeley 1967).

G. De Gaury, *Rulers of Mecca* (London 1951).

H. R. P. Dickson, *The Arab of the Desert: Glimpses into Badawin Life in Kuwait and Saudi Arabia* (London 1949); *Kuwait and her Neighbours*, ed. by C. Witting (London 1956).

D. Hawley, *The Trucial States* (London 1970).

D. Holden, *Farewell to Arabia* (London 1966) : Britain's withdrawal from the Arabian peninsula.

D. Hopwood (ed.), *The Arabian Peninsula* (London 1972).

H. Ingrams, *Arabia and the Isles* (3rd edn, London 1966) : the British administrator who helped to bring tribal peace to South Arabia.

T. Little, *South Arabia: Area of Conflict* (London 1968) : the troubled road to independence.

J. Marlowe, *The Persian Gulf in the Twentieth Century* (London 1962).

J. Morris, *Sultan in Oman* (London 1957) : a colourful portrait of a neo-medieval Arab ruler.

H. St J. B. Philby, *Saudi Arabia* (London 1968) : one of the greatest Arabian travellers.

R. Sanger, *The Arabian Peninsula* (Ithaca, N.Y. 1971).

H. Scott, *In the High Yemen* (London 1942).

K. S. Twitchell, *Saudi Arabia* (3rd edn, Princeton 1958).

M. W. Wenner, *Modern Yemen 1918–66* (Baltimore 1967) : a useful study of a rare subject.

Egypt

A. Abdel-Malek, *Egypt, Military Society* (New York 1968) : a contemporary Egyptian Marxist's account.

E. Baring (1st Earl of Cromer), *Modern Egypt*, 2 vols (London 1908) : the real ruler of Egypt, 1883–1907.

J. Berque, *Egypt, Imperialism and Revolution* (London 1972) : the social history of Egypt during the period of British domination and occupation.

M. Colombe, *L'Évolution de l'Égypte 1923–50* (Paris 1951): Egypt under parliamentary government.

B. Hansen and G. A. Marzouk, *Development and Economic Policy in the U.A.R.* (Amsterdam 1968).

H. E. Hurst, *The Nile* (London 1952) : a classic study of the river which is the basis of Egypt's existence.

C. Issawi, *Egypt at Mid-Century* (London 1954). *Egypt in Revolution* (London 1963) : an economic analysis.

J. and S. Lacouture, *Egypt in Transition* (London 1958) : two French writers' account of the first post-revolutionary years.

T. Little, *Modern Egypt* (London 1967).

Lord Lloyd, *Egypt since Cromer* 2 vols (London 1934) : Britain's imperial-minded High Commissioner in Egypt 1925-9.

K. Love, *Suez, the Twice-Fought War* (London 1969) : a detailed study of the origins and effects of the 1956 and 1967 wars.

P. Mansfield, *Nasser's Egypt* (2nd edn, London 1969).

J. Marlowe, *Anglo-Egyptian Relations 1800-1953* (London 1953).

R. P. Mitchell, *The Society of the Muslim Brothers* (London 1969).

A. Nutting, *Nasser* (London 1972) : a study by a former British minister who was closely involved in Anglo-Egyptian relations.

P. K. O'Brien, *The Revolution in Egypt's Economic System: from Private Enterprise to Socialism 1952-1965* (London 1966).

R. Stephens, *Nasser* (London 1971) : a full-scale biography.

P. J. Vatikiotis, *The Modern History of Egypt* (London 1969).

Iran

P. W. Avery, *Modern Iran* (2nd edn, London 1967).

A. Banani, *The Modernization of Iran 1921-1941* (Stanford, Calif. 1961) : the achievement of Riza Shah.

L. Binder, *Iran: Political Development in a Changing Society* (Berkeley 1962).

Cambridge History of Iran, vols i–v (Cambridge 1968) : vols vi–viii in preparation.

G. N. CURZON (1st Marquess Curzon of Kedleston), *Persia and the Persian Question*, 2 vols (London 1892) : the British Viceroy of India 1898–1905 and Foreign Minister 1919–24.

R. W. COTTAM, *Nationalism in Iran* (Pittsburgh 1964).

L. P. ELWELL-SUTTON, *Persian Oil: A Study in Power Politics* (London 1955) : a pro-nationalist account of the Persian oil crisis.

A. K. S. LAMBTON, *Landlord and Peasant in Persia* (London 1953); *The Persian Land Reform 1962–1966* (Oxford 1969) : two excellent accounts.

G. LENCZOWSKI, *Russia and the West in Iran 1914–48* (Ithaca 1949).

A. C. MILLSPAUGH, *Americans in Persia* (Washington 1946): the American administrator-general of Persian finances 1922–7 and 1943–5.

SIR PERCY SYKES, *History of Persia*, T *vols* (3rd edn, London 1930).

Iraq

LORD BIRDWOOD, *Nuri es-Said* (London 1970) : biography of Iraq's dominant political figure 1930–58.

U. DANN, *Iraq under Qassem: A Political History 1958–1963* (London 1969) : the first five years of the Iraqi Republic.

C. J. EDMONDS, *Kurds, Turks and Arabs* (London 1957) : the three main racial strains in Iraq.

H. A. FOSTER, *The Making of Modern Iraq* (London 1936).

I.B.R.D., *The Economic Development of Iraq* (Baltimore 1952).

M. KHADDURI, *Independent Iraq 1932–1958* (2nd edn, London 1960); *Republican Iraq: a Study in Iraqi Politics since the Revolution of 1958* (London 1958).

K. HASEEB, *The National Income of Iraq 1953–1961* (Oxford 1964).

S. LLOYD, *Twin Rivers: A Brief History of Iraq from the*

Earliest Times to the Present Day (London 1945) : a famous archaeologist's history.

S. H. LONGRIGG, *Iraq, 1900 to 1950* (London 1953).

E. MAIN, *Iraq from Mandate to Independence* (London 1935) : Iraq under British control.

J. A. SALTER, (1st Baron Salter of Kidlington) and S. W. PAYTON, *The Development of Iraq* (London 1955).

Israel/Palestine

N. BARBOUR, *Nisi Dominus: A Survey of the Palestine Controversy* (Beirut 1969) : the Palestine problem until 1945.

M. BAR-ZOHAR, *The Armed Prophet: A Biography of Ben-Gurion* (London 1967) : the life of Israel's first prime minister.

E. AGRESS, *Golda Meir* (London 1969).

N. BENTWICH, *Israel: Two Fateful Years 1967–69* (London 1969).

J. H. DAVIS, *The Evasive Peace: A Study of the Zionist–Arab Problem* (London 1968).

S. N. EISENSTADT, *Israeli Society* (London 1969).

B. HALPERN, *The Idea of the Jewish State* (Cambridge, Mass. 1961).

D. HOROWITZ, *The Economics of Israel* (Oxford 1967) : a survey by the Governor of the Bank of Israel.

D. INGRAMS (ed.), *Palestine Papers 1917–1922: Seeds of Conflict* (London 1972).

J. MARLOWE, *The Seat of Pilate* (London 1959) : a general account of Britain's mandate in Palestine.

E. O'BALLANCE, *The Arab-Israeli War 1948* (London 1956) : a military study.

A. PERLMUTTER, *Military and Politics in Israel: Nation-Building and Role Expansion* (London 1969) : the role of the army in Israeli political life.

L. STEIN, *The Balfour Declaration* (London 1961).

C. SYKES, *Crossroads to Israel* (London 1965) : a detailed study of the events leading to the creation of Israel in 1948.

Jordan

A. DEARDEN, *Jordan* (London 1958).
J. B. GLUBB, *The Story of the Arab Legion* (London 1948) :
   by the former British commander of the Legion.
G. L. HARRIS, *Jordan: Its People, its Society, its Culture*
   (New Haven, Conn. 1958).
I.B.R.D., *The Economic Development of Jordan* (Baltimore
   1957).
P. J. VATIKIOTIS, *Politics and the Military in Jordan: A
   Study of the Arab Legion 1921–1957* (London 1967) : the
   role of the army in Jordan.

Libya

E. E. EVANS-PRITCHARD, *The Sanusi of Cyrenaica* (Oxford
   1963) : an anthropological-historical study.
A. PELT, *Libyan Independence and the United Nations*
   (New Haven, Conn. 1970) : how a united Libyan state
   was created.
J. WRIGHT, *Libya* (London 1969).

The Maghrib: (i) General

J. M. ABUN-NASR, *History of the Maghrib* (Cambridge
   1971).
S. AMIN, *The Maghreb in the Modern World* (London
   1970) : French colonisation and independence from a
   Marxist standpoint.
J. BERQUE, *French North Africa* (London 1967).
W. KNAPP (ed.), *A Survey of North-West Africa* (London
   1973).

The Maghrib: (ii) Algeria

I. CLEGG, *Workers' Self-Management in Algeria* (London 1971) : a study of Algeria's socialist experiment since independence.
Y. COURRIÈRE, *La Guerre d'Algérie*, 4 vols (Paris 1968–71) : a balanced and detailed history of the Algerian Revolution.
G. ESQUER, *Histoire de l'Algérie 1830–1960* (Paris 1960) : a concise survey in the 'Que sais-je?' series.
E. F. GAUTIER, *L'Evolution de l'Algérie de 1830 à 1930* (Algiers 1931) : the classic justification of French rule.
A. NOUSCHI, *La Naissance du Nationalisme algérien* (Paris 1962) : well-documented left-wing account.
D. and M. OTTAWAY, *Algeria: The Politics of a Socialist Revolution* (Berkeley 1970).
D. PICKLES, *Algeria and France, from Colonialism to Co-operation* (London 1963).
W. D. QUANDT, *Revolution and Political Leadership: Algeria 1954–1968* (Cambridge, Mass. 1969).

The Maghrib: (iii) Morocco

A. AYACHE, *Le Maroc: Bilan d'une Colonisation* (Paris 1956).
N. BARBOUR, *Morocco* (London 1965) : a general introduction.
R. BIDWELL, *Morocco under Colonial Rule* (London 1973) : French administration of tribal areas 1912–56.
ALLAL FASI, *The Independence Movement in Arab North Africa* (Washington 1954) : by the veteran Moroccan nationalist leader.
R. LANDAU, *Moroccan Drama 1900–55* (London 1956) : the French and Spanish Protectorates.

J. L. Miège, *Le Maroc* (Paris 1950) : a concise survey in the 'Que sais-je?' series.

R. Montague, *Les Berbères et le Makhzen dans le Sud du Maroc* (Paris 1930).

A. Scham, *Morocco: Lyautey in Protectorate Administration 1912–25* (Berkeley 1970).

The Maghrib: (iv) Tunisia

A. Demeersman, *Tunisie, Terre d'Amitié* (Tunis 1955) : pre-independence introduction.

F. Garas, *Bourguiba et la Naissance d'une Nation* (Paris 1956) : a popular biography of Bourguiba.

W. Knapp, *Tunisia* (London 1970).

A. Raymond, *La Tunisie* (Paris 1961) : a good short summary in the 'Que sais-je?' series.

P. Sebag, *La Tunisie* (Paris 1951) : a Marxist account.

Salaheddine Tlatli, *Tunisie nouvelle* (Tunis 1957) : a Tunisian account.

Syria and the Lebanon

K. S. Abu Jaber, *The Arab Ba'th Socialist Party* (New York 1966).

R. Fedden, *Syria* (London 1946) : a colourful portrait.

P. K. Hitti, *Syria: A Short History* (London 1959) : from ancient Semitic times to the present.

A. H. Hourani, *Syria and Lebanon: A Political Essay* (London 1946) : the best interpretation of the French Mandate.

M. C. Hudson, *The Precarious Republic: Political Modernization in Lebanon* (New York 1968).

H. Lammens, *La Syrie*, 2 vols (Beirut 1921) : Syria before the French Mandate.

S. H. Longrigg, *Syria and Lebanon under French Mandate* (London 1958).

E. Rabbath, *Unité Syrienne et Devenir arabe* (Paris 1937) : a nationalist view.

Pierre Rondot, *Les Institutions politiques du Liban* (Paris 1947).

K. S. Salibi, *The Modern History of Lebanon* (London 1965) : a Lebanese historian's account.

N. A. Ziadeh, *Syria and Lebanon* (London 1957).

Turkey

F. Ahmad, *The Young Turks: The Committee of Union and Progress in Turkish Politics 1908-1914* (Oxford 1969) : a good account of the Young Turk movement.

J. C. Dewdney, *Turkey* (London 1971) : a geographical study.

Z. Y. Hershlag, *Turkey: The Challenge of Growth* (Leiden 1968) : an economic assessment.

I.B.R.D., *The Economy of Turkey* (Baltimore 1951).

Lord Kinross, *Atatürk: The Rebirth of a Nation* (London 1964) : the standard western biography of Atatürk.

B. Lewis, *The Emergence of Modern Turkey* (2nd edn, London 1968) : an excellent account of the origins and development of the Turkish Republic.

G. L. Lewis, *Turkey* (3rd edn, London 1965).

L. V. Thomas and R. N. Frye, *The United States and Turkey and Iran* (Cambridge, Mass. 1952).

A. J. Toynbee, *The Western Question in Greece and Turkey* (London 1923).

5. JOURNALS

The following deal wholly or partly with the Middle East : *International Affairs* (quarterly) and *The World Today* (monthly) : published by The Royal Society for International Affairs, London.

International Journal of Middle East Studies (quarterly : Cambridge 1970–).
Middle East International (monthly : London 1971–).
Middle East Journal (quarterly : Washington 1947–).
Middle Eastern Studies (thrice yearly : London 1964–).
New Middle East (monthly : London 1970–).
Journal of Palestine Studies (quarterly : Beirut 1971–).
L'Orient (quarterly : Paris 1957–).
Oriente Moderno (quarterly : Rome 1921–).
See also Palestine Monographs of the Palestine Research Centre, Beirut.

Index

France, 8; takes Algeria and
Tunisia, 11; Moroccan Protectorate (1908), 31; Sykes–
Picot Agreement, 44;
occupies Syria and Lebanon,
46; mandates, 54; Grand
Liban created, 55; policy in
Syria and Lebanon, 73–6,
94–5; and Algeria, Tunisia
and Morocco, 102–4; 1956
attack on Egypt, 122; leaves
Tunisia, 136–7; agrees to
Moroccan independence,
138; Algerian independence,
138–41
Fuad, Sultan of Egypt, 59;
King, 62, 80

Gailani, Rashid Ali: and the
'Golden Square', 95–6
Gaulle, General Charles de, 93;
policy in Algeria, 140
Gaza Strip, 111; Israeli raid on
(1955), 119
Germany: military aid to
Turkey, 21; policy in Middle
East, 22–3
Ghazi, King of Iraq, 77–8
Gladstone, William, 11 n
Glubb, General John Bagot,
British C.-in-C. Arab Legion:
dismissed by Jordan, 120
Goltz, Colonel von der, German
military adviser in Turkey,
21–2
Gorst, Sir Eldon, Consul-
General in Egypt, 31, 60
Gouraud, General Henri
Eugène, 54; decree of (1920),
55
Greco-Turkish War (1920–2),
65
Greece, 5; ambitions in Turkey,
65
Gulf, Persian: British treaties
in, 12; British withdrawal
announced (1968), 157

Habbash, George, leader of
P.F.L.P., 154
Haganah (Jewish secret army),
90
Hamid II, Abdul, Sultan of
Turkey, 14; policy, 15–16;
and religion, 19–20; internal
policy, 21–2; overthrown,
23–4; counter-revolution
attempt, 27; deposed, 27
al-Hasa: Turkish occupation
(1871), 16; Arab seizure of,
30
Hassan, Moulay, 17
Hassan II, King of Morocco,
liberalisation policy, 163
Hejaz (western Arabia), 1, 16;
Railway, 20, 30; under
Hussein, 58
Helleu, General: British
ultimatum to, 94
Histadruth, Jewish trade union
confederation, 90
Hogarth, Commander D. G.,
assurances to King Hussein,
50–1
Hourani, Akram, Syrian
politician, 125
Hussein, Amir Ibn Ali: Sharif
of Mecca, 30; and First
World War, 36–7; negotia-
tions with Kitchener, 37;
McMahon correspondence,
39–42; King of the Hejaz,
43; fears British support of
Jews, 50; abdication, 58
Hussein, King of Jordan:
dismissal of General Glubb,
126; coup against own pro-
Nasser government, 127

Ibn Rashid, Ruler of Shammar,
16, 37, 43
Ibn Saud, Abdul Aziz, 30, 37;
treaty with British, 38; defeat
of Hussein – King of the
Hejaz (1926), 58; King of